ADVANCE PRAISE

"Change isn't slowing down, it's speeding up. To keep pace, we can't rely on the mindset and behavior of the past to succeed in the future. Accelerated is packed with real case studies, methods, and models to help you navigate uncertainty and leverage the forces of accelerated change. If you're seeking to invent the future, and not fear it, read this book."

—BARRY O'REILLY, CO-FOUNDER OF NOBODY STUDIOS, FOUNDER OF EXECCAMP, AND BESTSELLING AUTHOR OF *UNLEARN* AND *LEAN ENTERPRISE*

"Every so often a book comes along that is exactly right for the moment. Brian Ardinger's new book, Accelerated, is a clarion call for optimism. You can learn to move faster and create the future rather than feeling like a victim of it. A great read."

—RITA MCGRATH, AUTHOR OF *SEEING AROUND CORNERS*

"Brian Ardinger is training the next generation of Accelerators to become better builders, makers, movers, shakers, founders, and creators. *Accelerated* offers quick, simple, and effective ways to impact the future of any organization."

—DIANA KANDER, *NEW YORK TIMES* BESTSELLING AUTHOR OF *ALL IN STARTUP*

"Brian Ardinger thrives at the intersection of corporate and startup innovation. His pragmatic approach in *Accelerated* will help you gain momentum while reducing uncertainty."

—DAVID BLAND, BESTSELLING AUTHOR OF *TESTING BUSINESS IDEAS*

"*Accelerated* is packed with tools designed to get you up to speed quickly so you can have more impact in less time."

—JACK ELKINS, FOUNDER OF SIDEKICK INNOVATION AND FORMER DIRECTOR OF INNOVATION FOR THE NBA'S ORLANDO MAGIC

"Brian Ardinger captures his extraordinary talent as a business mentor between the covers of this fantastic book. *Accelerated* is a must-read for anyone building a new business in our complex and uncertain world."

—CHRIS SHIPLEY, CO-AUTHOR OF *THE ADAPTATION ADVANTAGE*

"Brian Ardinger sounds the alarm, and rightfully so, that too many organizations are not set up to truly innovate. He provides a number of great case studies, along with personal stories of his own experience with startups and corporate innovators that will have you nodding 'yes, yes, yes' and wanting to effect change as fast as possible. Read the book, then go out and do stuff."

—BEN YOSKOVITZ, CO-AUTHOR OF *LEAN ANALYTICS*
AND FOUNDING PARTNER AT HIGHLINE BETA

"In today's world of hyper-uncertainty, we need better ways to explore, engage, and experiment with our ideas to turn them into valuable innovations. Accelerated gives you a front-row seat for how to do this."

—JOSH LINKNER, *NEW YORK TIMES* BESTSELLING
AUTHOR, FIVE-TIME TECH ENTREPRENEUR,
AND VENTURE CAPITAL INVESTOR

"Brian Ardinger has been helping both entrepreneurs and corporate innovators navigate the new world of innovation. His latest book, Accelerated, tackles the core obstacles and opportunities inside and out."

—SEAN AMMIRATI, COFOUNDER AND DIRECTOR
OF CMU CORPORATE STARTUP LAB

"For any entrepreneur or corporate innovator hoping to better their innovation acumen, Accelerated is a must-read."

—TENDAYI VIKI, AUTHOR OF *PIRATES IN THE NAVY*

"There's a lot of innovation theatre in modern business— companies doing Agile and Lean, without actually knowing what that means. In Accelerated, Brian draws on decades of experience to show what great accelerators actually do: take an early idea to a sustainable, repeatable business model by learning and iterating."

—ALISTAIR CROLL, CO-AUTHOR OF *LEAN ANALYTICS* AND *JUST EVIL ENOUGH*

ACCELERATED

ACCELERATED

A GUIDE TO INNOVATING AT THE SPEED OF CHANGE

BRIAN ARDINGER

FOUNDER OF INSIDE OUTSIDE INNOVATION

LIONCREST
PUBLISHING

ACCELERATED

A Guide to Innovating at the Speed of Change

FIRST EDITION

ISBN   978-1-5445-3199-1   *Hardcover*

978-1-5445-3198-4   *Paperback*

978-1-5445-3200-4   *Ebook*

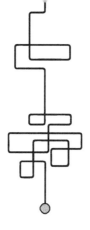

CONTENTS

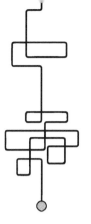

INTRODUCTION

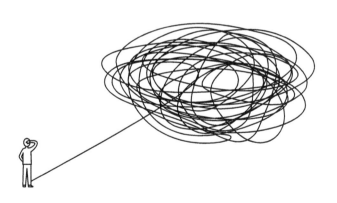

In 1955, Fortune magazine published its first Fortune 500 list ranking the largest companies in America. The list has become synonymous with business success. Yet only 10 percent of the companies on the original list remain on it today. It only took a few decades for 90 percent of the best companies in the world to become displaced—bankrupted, merged, contracted, or reorganized.

Fast forward to today. The rise of new technologies, a changing workforce, dynamic market models, geopolitical conflicts, and a global pandemic are colliding. The current climate of displacement is even more accelerated. Access to information is doubling, while the half-life of marketable skills is shrinking. The consulting firm Innosight estimates that the current pace of disruption will replace half of today's S&P 500 firms over the next ten years.

We live in a world of accelerated change, and every individual and organization that can't keep up is at risk. If you're a business executive, team leader, or startup founder, you're probably asking, "How do we create and grow value in an environment of constant uncertainty? How do we do so at ever-increasing speeds?" This book will help answer these questions and better prepare you to adapt to and act on whatever comes next.

Thriving amidst accelerated change requires quickly transforming new ideas into impactful outcomes. It requires letting go of the business-as-usual, slow-and-steady pace of the past. It requires innovating at the speed of change.

ACCELERATING INNOVATION IN AN ACCELERATED WORLD

Most people associate innovation with the invention or creation of something brand new, like the airplane or the light bulb. That is only one kind of innovation. Innovation in its simplest form is the process of transforming an idea into something of value. In this regard, you don't need to be a mad genius to innovate. Anyone can do it. Find a problem, solve the problem, and create value along the way.

Innovation starts with ideas. Ideas are everywhere, but ideas aren't enough. To innovate, we need to explore, refine, and turn our ideas into valuable outcomes. And in today's environment, it's imperative to do this quickly and effectively. We need to become great at accelerating innovation.

This book outlines the transformation process from idea to innovation. It's for anyone who needs to adapt, change, and deliver new products, new value, and new initiatives. It's a quick start guide for growth and a handbook for accelerating innovation in an accelerated world.

Over the last twenty-five years, I've helped startups and corporate innovators develop better ways to launch new ideas and compete. I've seen firsthand how people grow and adapt to an ever-increasing array of change and disruption. I've learned from investing in startups, training corporate innovators, and working with C-suite executives on the changing role of technology, startups, innovation, and the future of work. My work inside and alongside prominent corporations and the latest startups has given me a front-row seat to the process of turning new ideas into innovation.

I began my career in Asia–Pacific and Silicon Valley with Gartner, working with legendary technology clients like IBM, HP, and Microsoft. During the early days of the dot-com era, I led the research group at a high-growth startup that created Asia's first dedicated usability lab—where we developed the Web's early infrastructure for companies like HSBC Bank and Cathay Pacific Airlines. I returned to the US to work with a startup that was building software solutions for notable brands like Nike, Pepsi, Apple, Target, Royal Caribbean, and Harley-Davidson.

I later founded the NMotion startup accelerator and InsideOutside.io, the innovation consultancy and community I still run today. In addition to my own hands-on experience, I've studied and compiled lessons from leaders in innovation and entrepreneurship. I've interviewed hundreds of founders, investors, entrepreneurs, and corporate leaders for our weekly *Inside Outside Innovation* podcast. And I've hosted thousands of new innovators as part of our IO Summit events and Inside Outside Innovation community.

Currently, I lead a team of innovation advocates at Nelnet, a publicly traded company with over nine thousand employees. My role is to help drive innovation inside and outside the company, including investing in startups as part of our corporate venture capital arm and consulting, training, and coaching our many diversified business units in the tactics and culture of accelerated innovation.

Seeing all this firsthand has convinced me that if you're not learning and building innovation skills every day, you and your organization won't keep up and grow as needed. You will end up taking the slow, or more likely rapid, march toward irrelevance.

I've designed this book to give you context for the changing landscape of innovation and offer some tools and tactics to create better builders, makers, and idea accelerators to help you avoid the fate of so many others who failed to adapt and innovate.

Let's get started!

CHAPTER 1

THE RISE OF THE INNOVATION ACCELERATOR

The skills to navigate accelerating change and quickly adapt to what's coming next will be most important in creating value for yourself and your organization. They will also be the most sought-after skills. Those who develop these superpowers to embrace the breakneck pace and create new value will join the ranks of the business world's modern-day superheroes, known as "The Innovation Accelerators."

An Innovation Accelerator is a builder, maker, mover, shaker, founder, or creator. An Innovation Accelerator's job is to explore and experiment in unknown, uncertain, and ever-changing environments. They can take an idea and expeditiously transform it into reality—finding and creating value from the new and unknown. They navigate ambiguity, overcoming the instinct for more clarity and assurance, and are comfortable with not knowing what's ahead. They move forward with confidence, even without complete information.

Innovation Accelerators come in various packages. They are startup founders launching new experiments, product teams solving customer problems, and enterprise leaders adapting and growing as the world shifts beneath them. **Anyone with the ability to explore, engage, and experiment with new ideas to create valuable outcomes can become an**

Innovation Accelerator. Organizations will rise and fall based on their talent stack of Innovation Accelerators. Communities will grow and thrive based on their population of Innovation Accelerators. And your career growth and success will be influenced by your Innovation Accelerator skillset.

THE SEVEN SUPERPOWERS OF INNOVATION ACCELERATORS

I've worked with many Innovation Accelerators, from startup founders to community leaders. The following are the prevalent skills they possess—skills you too can develop to foster innovation competency in yourself and others. I call these superpowers the Accelerator Seven.

- **Curious.** Always on the hunt for the new and novel—driven by a quest for learning. They have a knack for asking questions and exploring areas beyond what they know or understand.

- **Optimistic.** Looking for the good and asking "what if?" and "why not?" questions. They understand that mistakes and failure are part of the process. They don't dwell on the negative, and they look for ways to overcome downsides.

- **Resourceful.** Knowing how to make a dollar stretch and make the most of the resources around them. They are good at asking for help and aren't afraid to get creative when needed.

- **Resilient.** Understanding the landscape of change and uncertainty and realizing that not everything will go according to plan. They can pivot and persevere when challenges and blockers appear, and they have the grit and determination to move forward continually.

- **Customer Driven.** Understanding and serving their customers. They can feel their pain points and empathize with their customers' challenges and opportunities.

- **Action Oriented.** Taking action. They get the ball moving, make decisions, and make consistent progress. They prefer to learn from the results of their actions. They test and experiment and are comfortable being wrong.

- **Collaborative.** Knowing that innovation is a team sport. They rely on collaboration with their network, always ask for help and insights, and lean on experts to increase their learning and progress.

These superpower skills enable Innovation Accelerators to take their ideas and create valuable innovations. But before we get to "how" Innovation Accelerators do this, it's essential to understand the context of today's innovation environment.

FASTER CHANGES AND MORE IMPACT

For years we've heard about disruption—how new shifts impact a company that fails to innovate—and we've seen the examples: Kodak, Xerox, Nokia, Borders, Blockbuster. The list is long and growing. Disruption has always occurred. From the days of steam power to mass production to the internet to today, we've always had to adapt and innovate to changing times. ***The difference now is that changes are hitting us faster and with more impact than ever before.***

We've been conditioned to think that stability is normal and change is unusual. But, in industry after industry, we are finding that we are in a perpetual state of transformation. Skills, knowledge, and talent are all in play, and the pace is speeding up. Disruption is happening to individuals and organizations alike. Nothing will be immune from this accelerating change.

Optimizing and executing known business models works great until something significant changes. What worked in "known" environments seldom translates into a new and novel world. The trouble for most organizations is that the cycles of significant change are happening more frequently and more rapidly than in the past.

Organizations are not developing the systems and skillsets for a world that changes so quickly. The same holds for individuals. We fall into familiar patterns and old solutions. We fail to learn, unlearn, explore, or experiment. This failure to embrace innovation leaves us exposed and vulnerable to the ever-increasing speed of change. Accelerating change requires us to think and act differently. It requires us to understand and embrace innovation and its messiness.

In many ways, 2020 was the year most people finally understood the meaning of disruption. The COVID-19 pandemic was a rare point where everyone on the planet had to stop and restart in new ways, almost overnight. Accelerating changes came to everyone's doorstep and forced a reckoning: innovate, or risk getting left behind. Disruption moved from theoretical to ever-present in mere moments. Living in constant ambiguity and unknowns became the status quo, and opportunities to create or lose value materialized quickly.

And the pace continues today. Disruptive changes are coming at us faster and with more immediate impact. In the past, disruption was more isolated. It took longer for changes to spread. If you were a big company with time and resources, you could continue optimizing and rolling along.

Even before the pandemic, you could see the coming shift in speed and impact. Accenture analyzed 10,000 companies for a 2019 report and found that 71 percent were "either in the throes of, or stand on the brink of, significant disruption." That was *before* the disruption of COVID.

People and organizations with years of experience and practiced skillsets once had an advantage in preventing newcomers from catching up quickly. That advantage is shrinking. Accelerating change is impacting everything and everyone. There are plentiful opportunities to restart or reset for the new environment—to learn the skills and techniques necessary to grow in the face of uncertainty.

In the 1981 book *Critical Path*, Buckminster Fuller

introduced his "knowledge-doubling curve." The theory goes that until the year 1900, human knowledge approximately doubled every century. However, by 1950, human knowledge doubled every twenty-five years. In 2000, human knowledge would double every year. IBM expanded the prediction and estimated that, by today, knowledge would be doubling every eleven or twelve hours.

These changes have reset the game and moved everyone closer to the starting point. Old playbooks and rulebooks no longer apply the way they did before. But even though change has toppled the chess pieces, the playing field is now more level than ever.

Sustained volatility means anticipating and reconfiguring on the fly. You must build with volatility in mind rather than expect a stable environment with predictable inputs and outputs. How can you create new value in a consistent, evolving manner? Innovation is the key.

Old ways of linear thinking cannot keep up with today's exponential changes. The present is too fast and too complex, let alone the future. The only long-term competitive advantage lies in one's ability to explore, learn, and adapt. If you are to become an

Innovation Accelerator, you must become good at creating new value in new environments. Fast and flexible. Nimble or nothing. Accelerating innovation is the new imperative.

THE THREE ENGINES OF INNOVATION

Innovation is not a step-by-step, linear process. It's more like the process of digging around a cave looking for treasure or a way out. It's dark. It's unknown. Some caves have treasure, and some don't. There could be dangers or great rewards. But the only way to know for sure is to enter, explore, and experiment your way through the darkness.

To find value in the cave, your job as an Innovation Accelerator is to make decisions in unknown, uncertain, and ever-changing environments and navigate moving ideas to outcomes. The best Innovation Accelerators will be able to do this faster and more frequently.

The innovation process requires you to generate ideas, engage with them to refine and get feedback to determine which ones to pursue, and then experiment with moving the ideas forward faster.

There are three critical engines needed to accelerate

your innovation efforts: exploration, engagement, and experimentation. These engines are interconnected. Your job as an Innovation Accelerator is to fine-tune each engine to make sure you move your ideas along and enhance them along the way. I'll cover each engine in depth in chapters 4, 5, and 6, but here's a quick overview for now.

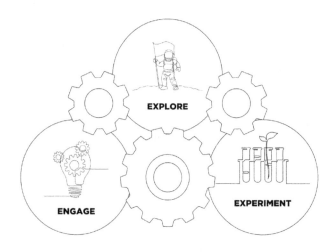

THE EXPLORATION ENGINE

The Exploration Engine is where you generate ideas, insights, and inputs, learn new things, unlearn old things, research, and find the patterns necessary to identify and understand opportunities at the earliest stages. The Exploration Engine is the engine that seeds the ideas you can then engage and experiment with. The more seeds you generate, the more ideas you can test, try, and eventually grow.

THE ENGAGEMENT ENGINE

The Engagement Engine is where you reflect and get feedback on the ideas and insights you gathered through exploration. It is where you identify, build, and utilize a collaborative network of people and resources to help you share and vet new ideas. The Engagement Engine sparks the seeds of your ideas, refines their value, and determines what you need to act on and explore further.

THE EXPERIMENTATION ENGINE

The Experimentation Engine is where you act on the ideas you found through exploration and refined through engagement. It's where you build, test, try, and learn. The Experimentation Engine is about incrementally moving ideas forward and creating valuable outcomes.

You must learn to utilize all three engines and acceler-ate the interactions between them. You should spend time each week conducting activities in each engine. I spend approximately 25 percent of my time in Exploration activities, seeding new ideas and looking for insights that can inform the ideas I'm working on. I spend another 25 percent of my time on Engagement activities, reflecting on what I found through Exploration and getting feedback and collaborative insights. I spend about 50 percent of a given week on activities related to Experimentation—acting on the ideas to try, test, build, and grow value. The amount of time you spend working on each engine will ebb and flow based on the number of ideas and the progress of each. The activities from one engine fuel and feed the other engines. Insights from Exploration feed Engagement and Experimentation. Results from Experimentation fuel further Exploration. The best Innovation Accelerators enable the engines to work together to create, build, and grow value.

If you can learn to explore, engage, and experiment, there is an immeasurable opportunity to create value faster and with more impact than ever before. Developing these innovation core competencies will enable you to impact the following groups:

- For customers, you'll be able to create better products and services with more impact.

- For employees, innovation will enable new opportunities, empowerment, and new rewards.

- For your organization, you'll be able to be more relevant, more competitive, and better positioned for change.

- For shareholders, innovation will pave a path for long-run growth and profitability, expanded market opportunities, cost savings and efficiencies, and more significant impact.

- And for you as an individual, having innovation as a core competency will strengthen your Accelerator Seven Superpowers to adapt and thrive.

In an era of relentless change, you need to accelerate your innovation efforts by moving ideas forward faster. You need to bring new ideas to life and create value along the way. Let's look at an example of a company that embraced the innovation imperative and an Innovation Accelerator mindset. The following is a case study of Domino's Pizza and its willingness to embrace and harness its engines of innovation—Exploration, Engagement, Experimentation.

DOMINO'S PIZZA: INNOVATION IN THIRTY MINUTES OR LESS

Domino's was founded in 1960. It grew over the years with a relentless focus on speed—optimizing cooking efficiency, delivery time, and increasing distribution. Domino's innovations and emphasis on speed and service led to groundbreaking moves that made it difficult for competitors to keep up. Remember their slogan, "30 Minutes or It's Free"?

Domino's grew into a multibillion-dollar business. But over the years, they made tradeoffs to optimize speed, sacrificing other factors, such as taste. Domino's had gotten good at optimizing everything *but* the pizza.

By 2008, amid a recession and facing a hyper-competitive mature industry, growth had stalled and prospects were dim. The things that used to work were no longer working. Domino's was facing increased competition, a ton of debt on its balance sheet, a record low share price of $2.83 per share, and a lack of new customers coming in the door.

Domino's had hit a wall. So, how do you reinvent a global pizza brand? How do you reinvent pizza? Innovation was the only way out. They needed to accelerate new ideas to create new outcomes.

First, they had to begin exploring and engaging with new ideas while fighting their internal fears. They had to overcome the fear of playing not to lose rather than playing to win and the natural inclination to be cautious, even in situations that demanded creativity and action. What if their actions would lead to even more significant problems than they had set out to solve? What if they lost their existing speed advantages and the pizza didn't improve?

They started exploring new ideas and insights by interviewing and engaging with their customers to understand their pain points. They realized they were solving the "Get me a pizza FAST" pain point but were leaving many customers behind by not solving the pain point of "I want a pizza that tastes good." They had open dialogues with customers, admitting that Domino's Pizza was crap, and they were on a mission to change it.

They began asking the "what if?" questions. *What if we can create a better-tasting pizza **and** capitalize on our expertise in speed and logistics?* They experimented with everything to develop a better tasting pie: sauces, toppings, crust, cheese. They tested over 7,500 combinations and experimented with supply chain, logistics, and marketing. They doubled down on technology as a differentiator. Of the 800 people working at its Ann Arbor headquarters, 400 work in software and analytics—not something that you would expect to improve pizza.

By the end of 2021, Domino's had grown its per share price to $564 and its market cap to $20.5 billion. Domino's completely realigned the perception of its product and its brand and innovated its way to becoming an e-commerce powerhouse and the most popular food delivery mobile app in the US by a significant margin. It continues to explore new ideas, engage with customers, and experiment with new offerings, such as ordering by texting a pizza emoji, or drone delivery. During the pandemic, to highlight the hefty fees restaurants pay for third-party delivery companies like DoorDash and UberEats, Domino's passed out gift cards of local competitor restaurants to its customers. CEO Patrick Doyle now calls Domino's a "technology-enabled, nimble, category disrupting machine."

I share this example because more and more companies (and individuals) will find themselves in similar shoes soon, having to adapt, change, and innovate to survive. Change and disruption are happening, and those who can build their skills and competency to innovate will have a better chance to thrive.

QUICK TAKES TO REMEMBER AND SHARE

- Changes are hitting us faster and with more impact than ever before.

- A failure to innovate leaves individuals and organizations more exposed and vulnerable to the ever-increasing speed of change.

- The ability to quickly adapt and create value from the new and unknown will be the skills of a new class of superheroes known as Innovation Accelerators. Your goal should be to grow these skills in yourself, your team, and your organization.

- An Innovation Accelerator's job is to explore and experiment in unknown, uncertain, and mutable environments. An Innovation Accelerator takes ideas and expeditiously transforms them into reality.

- There are three critical, interconnected engines needed to accelerate innovation: Exploration, Engagement, and Experimentation.

- An Innovation Accelerator's job is to fine-tune each engine to make sure ideas move forward faster to create new and valuable outcomes.

QUICK ACTIONS TO DO NOW

Accelerator Seven Superpower Skills
Self Scoring — How Did You Do?

On a scale from 1-10, rate your current abilities in each of the Accelerator Seven Superpower Skills.

	You	Your Organization
Curious		
Optimistic		
Resourceful		
Resilient		
Customer-Driven		
Action-Oriented		
Collaborative		
Total Points		

Excellent (63+ points)	You're You're Accelerated! You've got the chops to be a top-notch innovator and entrepreneur. Go out and innovate!
Good (49-62 points)	You're nearly there. Keep building and testing your innovation competencies!
Average (35-48 points)	Innovation is an ongoing process. You've come to the right place to continue learning some new tools and tactics.
In Need of a Booster (0-34 points)	Everybody's got to start somewhere, and innovation doesn't come easy. Now's the time to take steps to grow your confidence and skills.

THE FORCES OF ACCELERATING CHANGE

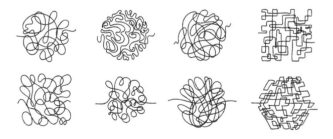

It's essential to understand the context of change and the forces that can either help or hinder your efforts to become an Innovation Accelerator. There are many forces driving today's accelerating pace of change. A single accelerant can have a massive impact in transforming your business, industry, or life. Today, however, multiple forces are converging at once. We need to understand these forces and leverage them to accelerate our ideas and innovations.

TECHNOLOGY

Technology may be the most significant accelerant of change and disruption, as well as an opportunity for growth. Technology is exponential and additive to the pace of change we're experiencing. Look at this sample of some of the new transformative technologies beginning to take shape.

Artificial Intelligence	Social/Mobile Internet
Autonomous Vehicles	Blockchain
Machine Learning	Cryptocurrencies
Computational Biology	NFTs
Robots	Biometrics
Big Data	Advanced Materials
Voice Technologies	Wireless Power
3D Printing	CleanTech
Beacons/RFID	AgTech
Chatbots	Quantum Computing
Nanotechnology	Drones
Advanced Genomics	Nanosatellites
Cloud Computing	Smart Cities
Wearables	Internet of Things (IoT)
Broadband/5G	VR/XR/Metaverse
GPT-3	mRNA

It's a long list. And we're just scratching the surface. Look at the list again. Which of these technologies are likely to impact your business or your career? Pick one, and chances are it will affect you and your industry, however tangentially. Most of these technologies are still nascent and evolving. What will be the effects of having all devices connected and embedded with intelligence? What about cheap, abundant energy sources? What happens when the human lifespan increases by ten or more years?

Look at the list one more time. Breakthrough technologies are being built not on a single technology but the combination of many of them. Even if you could pick one technology that would have the most impact, you can't escape the fact that all are hitting us simultaneously.

All of this results in the acceleration of more sophisticated technologies separated by shorter and shorter time intervals. New technologies are disrupting many industries at once. These technological advances are exponential, and humans are not good at comprehending exponential growth.

Technology is obliterating the current job landscape. A recent McKinsey study contended that by 2030, up to 40 percent of all workers in developed countries may need to upgrade their skillsets or seek new occupations. In the majority of US occupations, at least 40 percent of activities are automatable. In areas such as warehouse stockers and machine operators, the number is between 80–100 percent.

In every industry, technology is becoming more accessible and integral to all parts of a business. What used to be a specialized, vertical component focused on automation and optimization is now horizontal— no longer limited to an IT department. Salesforce made the sales function a technology function, from data analysis to prospecting to automation. In HR, technology affects everything from performance reviews to hiring to legal compliance.

New technology startups I've invested in, like Maptician, are changing space and office management, while Tilt makes it easier to manage employee leave. Logica is making financial forecasting accessible to the non-finance person. Companies like Slack, Zoom, Notion, Stripe, and others are redefining communication, infrastructure, operations, collaboration, and finance. Technology is now embedded and accelerating every business.

CAPITAL

In addition to advancing technological changes, access to capital is growing at record rates. It's also available to a broader swath of people than ever before.

The rise of access to risk capital is accelerating the number of experiments taking place in the market. More money means more opportunities for building, testing, and breakthroughs. We see growth in venture capital, private and corporate-based funds, and new capital models like crowdfunding. More money was raised by startups in 2020 during a pandemic than at any time in human history.

- Venture capital (VC) serves as startup or growth equity capital provided by private investors (angel investors, venture capitalists, and VC firms). This capital invests in innovation and growth at its earliest stages. Despite a pandemic, investments are higher than ever before, with nearly $130 billion invested in 2020. In 2021, the number increased to $329.9 billion across 17,054 deals, nearly doubling the previous annual record.

- Corporate venture capital (CVC) is a subset of the venture capital space. It is the practice of investing corporate funds into external startup companies. Led by massive CVC funds from Intel Capital, Google Ventures (GV), and Salesforce Ventures, more and more corporations are beginning to look outside to invest in startup companies as a source of innovation and protection against disruption. New corporate venture arms have reached record levels, tripling from 2011 to 2019, with investments soaring to over $73 billion in 2020.

- Innovators have access to new investment capital platforms like Kickstarter and Indiegogo, enabling startups, artists, and builders to source funds from early adopters, fans, and new customers. These crowdfunding platforms serve as an alternative to traditional financing options by tapping into a group's shared interest and bypassing the conventional gatekeepers and intermediaries required to raise capital. Funding can be a loan, an equity investment, a reward, or a pre-order purchase. The size of the global crowdfunding market is estimated to be over $100 billion. Corporations have begun to take advantage of this platform to test and experiment with real customers outside the traditional R&D route. Direct contact with the market is proving to be a game-changer for companies like General Electric and Whirlpool. They've used these platforms to prototype and gain market validation before spending money building and scaling production.

From private venture capital to corporate venture to crowdfunding, the dollars are growing to fund new ideas, new projects, and new innovations, accelerating the pace of change in the process.

MARKETS

Another source of acceleration is access to new markets. Before the internet and the advent of global communication and commerce platforms such as Facebook, Twitter, Google, Alibaba, or Amazon, a new company had limited ways to get in front of or interact with new customers. Businesses served limited geographical areas or spent massive advertising dollars to reach and promote to other markets. Niche markets were economically more challenging to aggregate and serve. Fast forward less than a decade, and now an early entrepreneur or innovator can reach any niche market worldwide for fractions of the capital or time once required. Needs for consuming new products are everywhere, and the means of production are there as well.

Alibaba's mobile app offers you access to manufacturing and production facilities to create virtually any product you can imagine from the comfort of your living room. Connect, communicate, design, price, manufacture, ship, and pay for all of it from the palm of your hand. We wanted to source backpacks for our Inside Outside Innovation Summit. I went on the app, chose from a half dozen manufacturers, submitted some specs and requirements, and started the process in seconds. The entire process was seamless. In less than sixty days, we created a unique product facilitated through technology and communication that even handled the cross-border financial, customs, and insurance aspects that would have taken an army of people and resources only a few years ago.

Another example of access to these platforms creating new opportunities for innovation is their ability to connect people and find other experts and resources at a fraction of the time and cost. Transparency and the ability to share knowledge and resources make it cheaper and easier to navigate new landscapes. Anyone with a smartphone today has access to all the world's knowledge. Want to learn how to grow a startup? You have direct access to the best and brightest in the world, on any topic you can imagine. You can learn about virtually any subject via YouTube.

Want a little more formality or credibility? Check out Udemy, Udacity, Khan Academy, MasterClass, LinkedIn Learning, Coursera, edX, and other online learning platforms.

Want even more access? Try connecting with the people directly. Communities on platforms like Reddit, Twitter, and Run The World are crawling with talent that anyone with a smartphone can engage with. I began my angel investing career by connecting via Twitter with interesting folks with knowledge and expertise. I was astonished at the access these platforms gave me to connect and cross-share skills and value. All you have to do is ask and do the work.

And it doesn't have to be only well-known "experts." Anyone can now find "pockets of value"—anyone with unique perspectives, insights, or knowledge. Anyone can begin conversations with early adopters, customers, and new markets. The ability to quickly and effectively access these pockets of value makes it easier for an individual to launch, test, and create new opportunities and innovations.

BUSINESS MODELS

The acceleration of new technologies, tools, and markets has enabled companies to explore and adopt new business models that change the landscape and upend the status quo.

A business model is the operating system of the enterprise. It is the pieces and parts of the organization, partners, and customers that come together to create, capture, and deliver new value for its stakeholders.

Alexander Osterwalder's Business Model Canvas identifies nine core components of a business model: cost structure, customer segments, value propositions, channels, customer relationships, revenue streams, key resources, key activities, and key partners. How these pieces are defined and how they interact with each other can change success and value creation. Technology has enabled the creation of many new business model opportunities. We can now do radically different things because of technological progress, globalization, deregulation, demographic shifts, and behavioral changes driven by these changes.

New business models can change an industry. Think Southwest's low-cost business model and its effect on the airline industry. Think Apple's iTunes App Store business model, which offers a marketplace platform for developers that Apple leveraged for a cut of everything sold on it. Think Salesforce and its business model innovation of delivering software as a service. Think Uber and its transportation model based on using other people's cars to operate. Think Netflix and the business model that leveraged new technologies to deliver content via the internet versus DVD and its latest move into content creation.

Emerging models like ghost kitchens (restaurants without brick-and-mortar locations) powered by influencer brands and the rise of delivery services can change the fast-food industry's production and consumption. Some facilities are made solely for producing virtual brands. YouTube star Jimmy Donaldson, known as MrBeast, an award-winning digital content creator, joined forces with Virtual Dining Concepts to create MrBeast Burger—a virtual restaurant brand. In December 2020, amid a global pandemic, the burger chain of 300 locations was launched overnight—something that took McDonald's six years to do. It sold over one million burgers with minimal infrastructure and operational overhead in its first two months. Launching such an initiative would not have been possible only a few short years ago.

These and other examples of new business model experimentation have unlocked billions of dollars of new innovation value. They have put competitive pressure on existing business models to remain optimized, efficient, and effective.

TALENT

Talent and ideas are everywhere—and becoming accessible to anyone. Even before the massive, simultaneous move of the majority of the world's workforce to remote during the COVID-19 pandemic, one of the biggest accelerants of change was the rise in access to talent anywhere.

The rise of startups and new ideas to incubate and quickly scale to become giants in their industry is accelerating the threats and opportunities. These changes have led to the ability to create disruptors. There's a rise of new startups grabbing the headlines and changing the status quo.

It used to take decades for companies to grow to disrupt an industry. We've seen that time shrink to a matter of years versus decades. Companies that used to take years to incubate can spin up an experiment in the market and scale faster than ever.

The ubiquity of today's collaboration tools, like Zoom, Slack, Dropbox, Evernote, and even the built-in capabilities of Apple, Google, and Microsoft's core tools, make it seamless to work from anywhere with anyone. Couple these tools with access to communities of talent like Fiverr, Upwork, Gigster, Asana, and Atlassian, and it's easier than ever to find, interact, hire, and engage with the best talent you can find and afford. The tools and tech have become so prevalent that it has created an entire freelance gig economy, whereby organizations and individuals contract with independent workers for short-term engagements.

Because of this, borders are less relevant. Find the best designer in Chicago, the best developer in Estonia, and the best data analyst in Mumbai. Collaborate. Shift and change teams as your needs grow or morph. Start small and scale fast. This flexible work environment is more of a reality today than ever before. Ideas and talent are distributed around the globe. My son is learning to program in the game engine Unity from a Latvian tutor over Zoom, and he found his next Blender instructor using the online talent marketplace Fiverr. This access to talent also means you are competing everywhere. Time to buckle up!

SKILLSETS

The half-life of your knowledge itself is shrinking. The skills that once set you apart are becoming less relevant. In many cases, the skills taught in school are irrelevant by graduation.

Because everyone is at the beginning of the learning journey, you can quickly become an expert and contributor in the new field. Technology skills, management skills, marketing skills, and HR skills are all changing. In a world of fast-moving change, there is a plethora of new topics, trends, and tools being introduced every week in which you can become an expert or contributor quickly. *New* is the default environment. Thus, everyone is a new learner in almost every area. Because of this rapid change, there are few areas where you have "missed the boat." And even if you have, there's a new boat on the horizon that you can grab.

Try it. Pick a new topic or trend that interests you. Dig in and get learning. A minimal effort in the new area will often give you outsized results versus an area already saturated with experts and known outcomes. You can apply this to any career or current area of expertise. There is always a new angle or trend that you can leverage in this manner.

I've used this technique often to build my career. Look for early trends or areas of interest. Jump in to learn a new space when things are beginning to develop, then leverage your knowledge into the new field. Rinse. Repeat. The technique can be applied in your existing field of knowledge to refresh and relaunch your expertise or in a new area of interest. The opportunities to use this technique will increase as the speed and intensity of change increase.

I used this approach when I started following the rise of the internet. I was early into UX and usability testing when developing the first dedicated research lab in Asia. I've followed my early interests and trends in customer experience software, startup ecosystems, angel investing, lean startup, podcasting, no-code, and corporate innovation. I've become connected and productive in all these areas by being early and active. If I'm doing it, others are too.

TOOLS

I'd venture to guess that you are within a few feet of your smartphone right now. That's a lot of power within your reach—power that wasn't accessible five or ten years ago.

What do you think all these tools in your pocket would have cost someone in 1985? $1,000? $20,000? In 1985, if you had access to all the technologies currently in your smartphone (the cameras, GPS, video, databases, music, etc.), the technology that now fits in your pocket would have cost about **$150,000**.

When you factor in the cost of computing power itself, you also would have needed a Cray supercomputer. Add in $32 million for that. Now, top that off with access to virtually all the world's knowledge at your fingertips, and you can begin to see the acceleration effects of everyone having access to these tools.

While only 0.5 percent of the people on the planet know how to code, new tools are democratizing access to technology, and innovation is on the rise. In addition to the smartphone, there is a growing number of NoCode/LowCode tools accelerating one's ability to create and build. The rise of these platforms and toolsets enables less technology-savvy users to develop applications and solutions without having a dedicated core programmer or development team. These tools will also free up current developers' abilities to tackle more significant and challenging coding initiatives.

I'm defining NoCode as off-the-shelf software, tools, and platforms enabling a nontechnical or less technical person to build, experiment, or pull together resources, data, and workflows to solve problems. NoCode brings drag-and-drop, copy-and-paste, and once complex capabilities to the masses. Tools like Bubble and Squarespace make website building easy. Airtable offers a no-code database and spreadsheet-on-steroids platform. Non-designers can use Canva to generate all varieties of marketing, promotional, and presentation assets that would have necessitated a multi-person marketing team in the past.

Creation generates creation. When you democratize the means of creation, you get more innovation as a result. When I started my career in technology in the mid-nineties, it was not out of the ordinary for companies to spend millions of dollars to launch a website. Not only did you have to develop the software, but you had to own the hardware, servers, database licenses, and everything else. Now you can launch an infinitely scalable site from virtually anywhere. Plus, you'll spend less than you would on a nice dinner (and accomplish it in about the same amount of time as it takes to eat one).

OTHER ACCELERANTS

The final forces of change are the rise of everything else that is uncertain and unpredictable. This category can include Black Swan events and other disruptors, be it geopolitical conflicts, political movements, coronavirus, or a myriad of other factors that individuals and organizations must navigate. These exponential changes are happening at multiple levels, accelerating innovation itself. While we can't always predict these accelerants, we must adapt to these unknown results and repercussions. The uncomfortable truth is that the only certainty is uncertainty.

The speed of change and its exponential nature have created a challenge and opportunity for individuals and organizations to learn new skills, master new mindsets, and prepare for new ways of thriving.

AIRBNB: LIVE LIKE AN INNOVATION ACCELERATOR

To see the impact of accelerating change, look no further than the rise of Airbnb, founded in 2008. Early on, while experimenting with the concept of renting out rooms in other people's houses, they funded their experiments by selling cereal boxes at the Democratic and Republican national conventions to keep the company going.

In a mere twelve years, Airbnb went from selling cereal to a valuation of over $100 billion. That's more than Marriott, Hyatt, and Hilton combined. They grew to have more rooms under management than Marriott and disrupted the travel industry.

Fast forward to 2020 and the onset of the COVID-19 pandemic. In just twelve weeks, everything shifted. Airbnb went from the doorstep of one of the most anticipated IPOs in 2020 to laying off 25 percent of its staff, having its valuation plummet over a third, and lacking any certainty that the travel industry would ever return.

Even an innovative company like Airbnb, which changed the dynamics of a centuries-old industry, was not immune from this pace of change. It managed to disrupt an industry in a dozen years and then encountered a similar fate in a matter of twelve weeks. Airbnb's ability to react and adapt again made it less vulnerable than many others in the industry suffering from the same disruption. It was built by entrepreneurs who still had a skillset and the mindset of innovators willing and able to quickly pivot and change based on market dynamics. Its ability to explore, experiment, and act on new alternatives with its customers and partners made it nimbler than legacy hoteliers.

Their reputation for innovation helped them IPO later in 2020. They closed the first day of trading at a valuation of $86.5 billion—more than Marriott, Hilton, and Intercontinental combined.

Disruption comes quickly. Whether it's twelve years or twelve weeks, similar scenarios like this continue to play out in every industry. Existing business models are being decimated and challenged. "Business as usual" is not an option.

QUICK TAKES TO REMEMBER AND SHARE

- There are many forces driving today's accelerating pace of change. A single accelerant can have a massive impact in transforming your business, industry, or life.

- Changes in technology, capital, markets, business models, talent, skillsets, tools, and many other areas are all converging.

- The speed of change and its exponential nature have created a challenge and opportunity for individuals and organizations to learn new skills, master new mindsets, and prepare for new ways of thriving.

- Disruption comes quickly. Whether twelve years or twelve weeks, examples like Airbnb continue to play out in every industry. "Business as usual" is not an option.

QUICK ACTIONS TO DO NOW

List the most significant forces accelerating change in your industry or life, such as technology, talent, regulation, and capital. Or maybe it's relationships, education, or skillsets. Begin to research and explore the challenges and opportunities these forces will create. What can you do now to better prepare for some of these changes?

CHAPTER 3

NAVIGATING
UNCERTAINTY

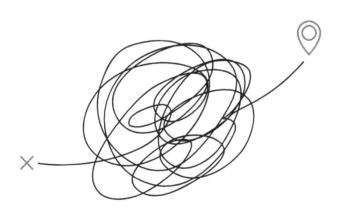

All this uncertainty is scary. No one wants to be looking over their shoulder, waiting for the next big thing to derail their plans. But if you can get better at adapting to change, today's uncertainty will turn into a massive opportunity.

The good news is that there are ways to leverage the accelerants of change in your favor. While scary, these changes open opportunities and usher in a new age of impact. Now everybody has access to the knowledge, tools, and skills to innovate and create new value. What once took large amounts of capital, people, and technology can be spun up in hours for next to nothing. Now a single individual has the tools and access to create and build something at a fraction of the time, cost, and effort. Accelerating uncertainty makes it possible to accelerate our engines of innovation. We can explore more ideas, engage more easily with talent and customers, and experiment using fewer resources.

While organizations feel this innovation imperative, the individual controls the ultimate outcome. Individuals within an organization are the ones who have an impact. We are seeing the "democratization of innovation," whereby everyone must become an Innovation Accelerator. Everyone can learn the skills and tools to navigate today's environment of persistent change.

The same accelerants that are changing organizations are creating opportunities for individuals to thrive and innovate. New technologies are providing new tools. New capital, markets, and talent are becoming available and accessible to everyone.

The ability to create value at a record pace and with record impact is now accessible to nearly everyone. The barriers to identifying, building, testing, proto-typing, and experimenting to solve problems have never been lower. Everyone is facing more challenges to solve, and everyone has more access to the tools and resources to solve them.

In the early 2000s, I ran a research division for a large web development company in Asia. We were building website infrastructure for companies like Cathay Pacific and HSBC Bank. We were studying how people used new internet technologies. We charged millions of dollars to build websites. It took hundreds of developers and months to create. It was painful and difficult. Now, a single person can create many of the same capabilities in minutes.

To scale and grow still takes time and money, but the immediate ability to start has never been easier or more accessible. The barriers decrease every hour as new tools are created, new markets are opened, and new lessons are shared. Learn to embrace this rapid change, and you too can have an impact.

So how do we adapt, grow, and thrive in a world of constant change and disruption? Everyone needs to develop a repeatable process for turning new ideas into new value creation. In Chapter 6, I'll outline the helpful 1-2-3-4 process developed at Nelnet and elsewhere. Building a competency of innovation is what sets people apart. We have the tools, tactics, and mindset for individuals and organizations to adapt to rapid change.

Despite the heartburn that uncertainty causes, it has several advantages for those trying to navigate it. To grow in this environment, we must learn to harness these benefits. Uncertainty...

- **...forces focus**. When faced with the unknown, you must concentrate and reevaluate what matters most and what needs to pivot or change. Uncertainty tends to highlight what's important.

- **...disrupts assumptions.** It causes us to unlearn what we thought we knew. It offers a reality check. It helps us rethink our assumed facts and challenges us to discover new ones.

- **...increases humility.** Uncertainty has a way of cutting down arrogance and intolerance. Being able to face uncertainty with "I was wrong about that" or "I'm unsure how to proceed" allows for a fresh look and a new start.

- **...forces action.** When we are too comfortable, we often fail to act. Why change when everything feels so good? Uncertainty is the opposite. It's uncomfortable and unenjoyable. Uncertainty forces us to act to avoid these feelings and resolve the tension.

- **...encourages gratitude.** There's nothing like a significant shift to cause you to give thanks for the things you have. In uncertainty, you can relish the advantages and benefits you can bring to solve the next challenge.

The best Innovation Accelerators will embrace innovation and use today's uncertainty to their advantage.

OVERCOMING BARRIERS TO ACCELERATED INNOVATION

If we know that change, disruption, and uncertainty are accelerating all around us, why are we not better prepared to handle it? While many forces are accelerating our need to adapt, there is also a host of barriers decelerating our ability to change and move quickly. The systems we've been using to manage, forecast, and deal with change are not keeping up. If we're playing by the old rules with old tools, we set ourselves up for failure.

Innovation is slowed when we navigate new territories with old maps. Our reliance on old maps, while perhaps directionally relevant, may not be applicable in uncharted territory. How do we continue to grow our existing businesses while also preparing ourselves for the new next? It's challenging to do and difficult to change overnight.

Most business leaders aren't comfortable in the realm of innovation. They can talk a good game about embracing innovation, but most have garnered success by executing and optimizing in known environments with known business models. Work the plan. Get the outcome you expect. This is the opposite environment of innovation.

Most innovation initiatives will fail unless we develop new mindsets and skills that work with the new, rapid-paced world. For someone who helps companies innovate, it's tricky to admit that most won't be able to do it. They can't help themselves.

In some ways, corporations are like world-class athletes. They're the best in the world at what they do. They know the rules and the competition better than anyone out there. They've optimized to maximize their muscles and perform at the highest levels.

But even the greatest athletes in the world can't switch and compete in a different sport overnight. Organizations are similar. "Switching games" can be done, but we need to train our innovation muscles as the new core competency. The Accelerator Seven Superpowers of being curious, optimistic, resourceful, resilient, customer-driven, action-oriented, and collaborative are necessary to adapt and respond to new rules and new opportunities. These are the competencies of innovation that we want to foster and grow. These competencies are the muscles that need to change when the time comes to play a different game.

Ironically, barriers to innovation often worsen the

more successful a company becomes. The bigger you are, the more likely you won't make it. Research from McKinsey suggests that 83 percent of all digital transformations fail, and the results are worse the bigger you are. Smaller companies (with fewer than one hundred employees) are 2.7 times more likely to report a successful digital transformation than larger organizations (with over fifty thousand employees).

While the path to innovation is difficult, at least there is a path. The alternative is to stand still and be overcome by the avalanche of exponential change, whether you're ready or not. As one CEO told me when I complimented him on his company's innovation efforts, "It's easier to innovate when there's a gun to your head." Some folks feel the pressure a little sooner than others. Rejecting innovation is often easier than embracing it. It takes both bottom-up and top-down culture, process, and robust leadership. But rejecting innovation is not an option.

To create an Innovation Accelerator organization, you must understand and overcome the common barriers and challenges faced during the innovation journey. Let's look at the issues that will slow down and derail your innovation efforts and what you can do to avoid them.

ENABLE INDIVIDUAL INNOVATORS

The first thing to understand is that organizations don't innovate. Individuals do. Organizations execute and optimize. Innovating means changing the status quo to create new value—to do something that adds or changes the existing value equation. Unfortunately, most existing systems are rigged against innovation by default.

Organizations hire optimizers and executors of the status quo, existing systems and business models. The systems are pulling in the wrong direction for innovation. HR hires talent to run an optimization engine. Talent is measured and rewarded to drive this engine. Compliance and Legal are there to protect and mitigate risk in the existing system. Organizations do not traditionally train individuals to innovate, nor reward or hire for innovation. An organization is doing what it has been designed to do when it *doesn't* innovate.

This focus on the existing business works when the underlying model doesn't need to change. As we've seen, though, this core assumption that companies can maintain the status quo long term is being challenged. Accelerating change forces companies to adapt sooner than desired or suffer the consequences.

Once you realize that the innovation journey will be difficult (and inevitable), it gives you a chance to push through the challenges that are bound to occur. I've found that embracing this fact helps companies begin the journey with a better mindset. It helps explain the obstacles faced and contextualizes the difficulty. It provides a window into why things aren't making progress. It allows you to redefine and reexamine what must happen to innovate.

To remain relevant, organizations must create an internal army of Innovation Accelerators with an environment to test, try, fail, and succeed. They must enable individuals to build a core competency of innovation. Corporate innovation works when individuals can drive innovation with the space to test, try, and learn to create new value. These individuals are the key to survival in the exponentially changing world.

Recognizing that the system will fight like antibodies to get rid of changes gives you a fighting chance to acknowledge these barriers and develop ways around them. If you build a company of Innovation Accelerators, they will innovate.

RELINQUISH THE LEGACY MINDSET

One of the most significant barriers to an organization's ability to innovate is a legacy mindset. We build systems and processes to protect and maximize the efficiencies of the existing business. We build organizations to exploit the status quo by default. These actions make sense and work great in slow-changing environments. As organizations grow, they hire experts and specialists to optimize areas further. Legal does everything to mitigate risk and protect the core. Technology creates processes to make things more efficient. Customers become tied to the brand and the legacy expectations.

Once an organization has moved from the startup exploration mode of finding a business model that works, it flips to become an optimizing machine. It can fall into the trap of only solving legacy problems for legacy customers. It is not looking at the new customer environment, technologies, or market dynamics. This legacy focus makes it difficult for organizations to "unlearn" or adapt to changes. "We know our customers. We know how to execute. We have a process for that. That's not what we do." These are the things you hear.

When change and uncertainty become the dominant

force in an existing market, organizations will need to continue to focus on executing and optimizing the existing business while also building an innovation engine that replaces the current business's value.

DEFINE A VISION FOR INNOVATION

A common barrier to innovation is not having a clear definition or context for innovation and its meaning to the organization. Some companies only think of innovation as new inventions or transformational ideas. Others think of innovation narrowly in the context of product enhancement only. Setting an innovation vision means looking at initiatives across a portfolio of activities and defining the areas to explore and pursue.

An excellent way to get an organization on the same page is to utilize some version of McKinsey's three horizons framework to help define innovation and determine how it fits into their existing and future business opportunities. To remain competitive in the long run, McKinsey's model suggests allocating a company's innovation resources across each of the following three horizons:

- Horizon 1 (H1) or "core innovations" are initiatives

that provide continuous innovations (improvements) to a company's existing business model. This "incremental" innovation creates value based on optimizing current products and services to existing customers and markets. Tremendous opportunities exist in finding and funding core innovations.

- Horizon 2 (H2) initiatives extend a company's current business model or core capabilities to new customers or new markets. These are "adjacent innovations," such as selling an existing product to a new market or selling a new product to the current market.

- Horizon 3 (H3) initiatives create new capabilities or new businesses to take advantage of or respond to market disruptors. H3 or "transformational innovations" are typically the hardest for existing organizations to execute or deliver. Ideas furthest from the core are riskier, unknown, and more challenging but have the potential for outsized rewards or protection against disruption. Because of the difficulty of H3 innovation, investing in and working with outside entities like startups or partners can often accelerate H3 value creation.

The three horizons model enables organizations to define and deliver innovation more broadly. It provides context to individuals for where innovation happens and offers an ability for more individuals to play a part in the innovation process.

Organizations should invest across all horizons of innovation—core, adjacent, and transformational. Often the vision for innovation is not bold enough or is unbalanced across the three horizons. Too many bets are placed in the more well-known or more easily measured areas of core innovation. If organizations aren't deliberate about the context of innovation and where they are placing bets and resources, it's easy to go off track.

Lack of vision is most often driven by fear. Fear of what happens if something doesn't work. Fear of the unknown. The early days of new ideas are a search process in an unfamiliar environment. Investor and founder of Y Combinator, Paul Graham, said, "The paths that lead to new ideas tend to look unpromising. If they looked promising, other people would already have explored them." In this context, it's a wonder that any innovations take place at all. Vision requires putting time, money, and resources toward an unknown and uncertain path that may or may not prove fruitful.

Since we can't predict the future, an innovation vision serves as a hypothesis of what we think the future might be. The hypothesis can evolve over time as it provides the glasses for the vision. It helps guide where the organization should be investing time and resources. It allows companies to clarify ideas, projects, and initiatives to explore and fund first. Since companies can't invest in every project or initiative, a clear innovation vision can guide the company and help direct finite resources.

An innovation vision can also head off political pet projects. It can limit nice-sounding presentations and help teams identify and pursue ideas in the organization's sweet spot rather than random, off-target acts of innovation.

DEMONSTRATE A SENSE OF URGENCY

Most organizations have a naive optimism that they can adapt fast if needed. We all too often hear excuses: "Our competitors are slow. It won't happen to us. We'll worry about that when the time comes." But innovation takes time, and companies can't change culture and processes overnight. It takes hundreds—if not thousands—of ideas to be filtered and experimented with to find the true game-changers. The faster companies can make innovation urgent, the more chances they may have to get it right. Rarely is a company entirely blindsided by innovation. Kodak invented the digital camera, and Xerox invented the graphical user interface, but each was slow to act on what they created. Urgency can be demonstrated by measuring and rewarding efforts around action and experimentation.

STOP TREATING INNOVATION AS A PROJECT

Innovation is not a one-and-done project. Innovation is ongoing. It is not something you launch, complete, and take off the list once it's "fixed." While individual initiatives can start and stop, innovation itself needs to be treated as an ongoing process of creating valuable outcomes from the new and unknown.

In good times, innovation is often funded and expanded by organizations. Innovation projects are launched, and all is well until the next business crisis or economic downturn. But when times get tough, companies often return resources (time, money, and attention) to the core. Innovation budgets get cut, and once again, individuals are reminded that innovation is not an integral part of the culture or future of the organization. When innovation initiatives are continually minimized or put on the backburner during difficult times, it can have long-term, damaging effects on retention, morale, and desire to innovate in the future. It can short circuit any value or momentum created by previous innovation initiatives. Don't fall into this trap. The bottom line is that if you want to innovate, you must make innovation a continuous focus area and a core part of an ongoing culture of value creation.

INCREASE YOUR RISK APPETITE

There are structural reasons why many breakthroughs come from individuals or startups outside rather than inside existing companies. Established organizations tend to be more cautious than their startup counterparts because they have more to lose. The pain of loss is more powerful than an unknown pleasure, and it often causes us to err on the safe side. Companies that play not to lose are over-cautious, fail to take risks, and miss out on opportunities. I've seen examples like not talking to customers for fear of damaging the existing brand or dismissing a new product idea based on early legal feedback without testing assumptions to see if the situation warranted it. Falling into these traps can lead us to worry more about taking action than doing nothing. Playing it safe or doing nothing is a risky proposition in disruptive environments.

There is an inherent fear of failure for existing organizations—a fear of losing what they already have. Startups have the opposite fear—fear of not succeeding. A startup's default state is failure with a goal to find success. With nothing to lose, startups fear the downside of not succeeding much more than losing something they don't have.

Most of the time, innovations within existing companies offer limited individual upside and downside risks. Suppose a person inside an organization creates a game-changer. In that case, they may move up the ranks or receive some bonuses, but the outsized benefits of building a business are not usually there. However, unlike startup founders building a company from scratch, the risks are reduced as well. A person building inside an existing company can lean on the company's regular paycheck, benefits, and resources that are unavailable to most startups.

The final difference is that a founder at a startup has the fundamental ability to change everything (or nothing). Autonomy to make the calls is inherently difficult for an inside founder. Inside innovators don't have the flexibility of a blank slate. Legacy brand, existing customers, and the need to protect the core business model is not something startups have to deal with initially. They also lack the flexibility to seek outside funding, partnerships, talent, etc., without approval from the mothership. Resources, partnerships, marketing, and pricing decisions all have the constraints of the core business to navigate.

IDEAS ALONE ARE NOT INNOVATION

Collecting ideas is not innovation. There are plenty of software platforms and options for generating, sorting, and prioritizing ideas from the crowd. You can google innovation management software (or find a list in our InsideOutside.io tools database) to review options like Ideawake, Brightidea, Spigit, Rever, Wide Ideas, and others. All offer a way to capture and prioritize ideas to give appropriate feedback. Most companies don't struggle with these tools or even with finding ideas, but rather with having the right processes and systems to turn these ideas into outcomes once the ideas are captured.

There are thousands of reasons why ideas stumble and fail. It's impossible at the earliest stages to know which ones will make it through the gauntlet.

Therefore, it is crucial to have a robust and ongoing pipeline of ideas to evaluate, vet, and try.

Companies need to broaden the number of ideas they try, test, and move forward (or kill them and move on to the next one). I've seen corporate innovators only fund a handful of ideas and expect to have one of them become an Uber or Airbnb in the process. While it can happen, the odds are you probably need to be funding hundreds.

Ideas also need to be sourced across the portfolio of many ideas. Ones close to the core business are likely to have more certainty and actionability with more immediate upside opportunities. Transformational or disruptive ideas may be riskier but may have more considerable outsized return opportunities (and may actually take less time to test, build, and implement than in years past due to the accelerating forces I outlined in Chapter 2).

LOOK OUTSIDE FOR ANSWERS

Believing that all innovation must come from internal sources is a significant barrier to innovation. Too few companies look outside their walls or industry for new or novel value creation. By default, digital transformations tend to look inward because individuals are trying to enhance their systems rather than looking outward for insights and answers. This approach might have made sense when the outside world was slow-moving. Now industry after industry changes rapidly. The number of new startups, technologies, and markets make it far more likely for a company with an excellent outside perspective to be able to leverage and learn at a much more rapid pace externally versus relying on a handful of individuals within its walls.

Looking outside also means engaging with your customers directly. It's easy to assume you know what's best without getting outside the building to validate, test, and learn firsthand from the market. My teams have fallen into this trap. Long before I began studying innovation, I was part of a software development team that spent $500K to build a new product that no one wanted. Worse than that, we spent almost a year before figuring out that we were on the wrong path. We were too dug into our assumptions and biases to realize there were alternatives if we had just gone outside to ask.

We made many mistakes along the way, but the biggest was not engaging with the market. We took too long and tried to be too perfect before letting our customers try it. We failed to anticipate market changes. We focused our time and energy on building features that no customer wanted. We assumed our sales reps had given us the correct insights about our customers' desires but never confirmed these assumptions. We failed to understand that our current customers were different from the potential customers for the new product. We waited too long to tap into our existing network of customers and partners. We moved slowly and methodically when the market and competitive demands required speed and iteration.

We executed a plan that we had developed and assumed as fact. We were in a land of uncertainty, acting like the outcomes we outlined at the beginning of the journey were wholly accurate. All we would need to do was execute the plan, and all would be well.

The product we made was quite good. Solid in its execution, user experience, and functionality. The trouble was that it wasn't a product anybody wanted. We became enamored with implementing and optimizing what we were building. We solved a problem that didn't need solving—at least, not to the degree and complexity we executed.

Since those days, I've seen far bigger mistakes repeated in organization after organization. Multiply these activities across project after project and company after company, and the loss of value adds up. You can avoid many of these issues by working on gaining an outside perspective.

STOP MISALLOCATING RESOURCES

Despite the accelerating pace of disruption, most organizations are not allocating enough resources to innovation—be it talent, training, or investments. Organizations should be spending resources on training individuals on innovation processes, hiring entrepreneurial talent, allocating new incentive systems, investing in internal and external startups, and other innovation initiatives.

In times of change and uncertainty, many companies divert innovation resources to fulfill short-term business demands. A recent Gartner survey reported that 80 percent of R&D leaders felt pressure to scale down or kill breakthrough projects in favor of more immediate priorities.

Worse, the ones that *are* investing are often misallocating resources. Too many provide sizable budgets with long timeframes and traditional milestones. They try to pick the "winners" and only invest in a few ideas. Organizations also overestimate the number of resources required to get an idea off the ground and allocate resources with the same infrastructure and specialization used to run their existing businesses. They think they need a team of specialists, a dedicated runway, marketing budgets, and infrastructure for any project regardless of the stage or viability of the idea.

The funding allocation process in venture capital and startups is one of my many takeaways from investing in startups that can apply to launching new ideas anywhere. An incremental, metered funding approach, as with venture capital, can be appropriate for early-stage innovation investing.

In this model, ideas are funded and built based on a team's ability to find traction and hit the next milestone. Investors incrementally fund startups to the next milestone, review their progress, and continuously bet on the ideas showing traction and growth. This stage-gated funding model enables oversight and incremental resource allocation through the uncertainty of launching and growing a new idea. Companies can use this same systematic approach to fund early ideas internally.

The good news is that the amount of resources required to get started has fallen dramatically. Given today's tools to prototype, test, and validate new ideas, it's never been easier for individuals with minimal budgets to get started. Once these new ideas show traction or support, they can be scaled and built out more robustly. Having the freedom and ability to test more ideas to find the ones that show promise is a massive advantage from years past.

MAKE INNOVATION IMPORTANT EVERYWHERE

Innovation cannot be someone else's problem to solve. Individuals and groups within the core business must embrace it. Innovation is not something that can happen "over there" or be "done" by someone else. Innovation needs to be an integral component of all parts of the organization.

I've seen many companies attempt to create stand-alone groups responsible for innovation efforts. These innovation hubs are designed and staffed to "do innovation." Business units throw ideas over to a small team to test and execute. People within the organization begin to look to the hub as "the place where innovation is supposed to happen."

Several problems can surface with this approach. The company cannot staff the hub to handle the number of ideas required to find enough breakthrough opportunities. The hub team rarely has the domain expertise of the core business that originated the idea in the first place. Therefore, the hub team has a steeper learning curve and uses more time and resources than it would have if the core team had vetted the idea themselves. Finally, once an idea does show some promise, it is difficult, if not impossible, to transfer the idea back to the core business. The handoff between the groups takes valuable time and resources, and frequently, the idea can never regain a good home to keep growing and moving forward.

MEASURE AND INCENTIVIZE INNOVATION

Among the most significant barriers to innovation are the metrics and incentive systems used to measure and motivate success—most incentives reward incrementalism and optimization, not exploration and innovation. While efforts to build and grow an existing business tend to offer more immediate results, without counter incentives to instill an appetite for innovation, organizations leave themselves open to missing outlier opportunities or failing to adapt to market changes.

When there are few incentives to innovate, you'll hear things like, "Now's not a good time for that," or "I've got too much on my plate to try/learn/do something new." An example of this is when I worked with a company to create an innovation training program similar to a startup community event called Startup Weekend. Startup Weekend, now run by TechStars, enables participants to pitch ideas, form teams, and see how far they can move that idea in forty-eight hours. The program gives participants a taste of what it's like to think, act, and move like a startup.

I developed a similar Startup Weekend–style event for employees to try as an innovation challenge. The biggest obstacle was finding time to allow employees to participate. While the company was saying they wanted to innovate, they were hesitant to take even a short amount of time to allow their employees a chance to do so. Ironically, when the event took place, one team created a software program that eliminated over $150K in annual licensing fees. A second team developed a new employee onboarding process that increased efficiency and likely saved millions. Allowing time to learn, test, and try new things is one of the most significant incentives a company can give to establish a culture of innovation.

Success in the future will require new skills for handling ambiguity, new technologies, and new business models. Yet most organizations don't have an "innovator's career path" or a way to learn these skills. Most organizations have no path to identify, measure, reward, track, evaluate, or think outside the core business path. Organizations preparing for new ways of work will need to build innovation competency into all career paths. Individuals with these skills will become more highly sought after and a more significant part of an organization's DNA.

Some incentives that are more aligned to fostering innovation can be bonuses tied to the number of ideas considered and vetted or the number of experiments run. Offering employees training and opportunities to develop their innovation muscles can also provide motivation. Recognizing those who incrementally build, test, try, and even fail can demonstrate that the company values these behaviors. Look for ways to reward the speed of learning. Incentivize teams to test assumptions in the market. Encourage action and experimentation.

FIGHT ORGANIZATIONAL ANTIBODIES

Most organizations have antibodies to resist change, and these antibodies can manifest themselves into challenges for the innovator. Internal politics can be a devastating barrier to accelerating innovation. The funding of pet projects, resource allocation, and subjective decision-making can impact the culture of innovation. To be an early innovator, you will take many arrows. Your projects may be undermined or sabotaged—sometimes directly, sometimes more subtly. You will feel it. You will be uncomfortable. But if you understand the context of where the fear is coming from and develop the skills and processes outlined in this book, you will be prepared to handle it.

If you're up for it, here's how you can take this journey. Even when organizations can't innovate, people can.

QUICK TAKES TO REMEMBER AND SHARE

- If we can better adapt to change, today's uncertainty will turn into a massive opportunity.

- The ability to create value at a record pace and with record impact is now accessible to nearly everyone. The barriers to identifying, building, testing, prototyping, and experimenting to solve problems have never been lower.

- While many forces are accelerating our need to adapt, there are also a host of barriers decelerating our ability to change and move quickly.

- Most organizations have succeeded by executing and optimizing in known environments with known business models. But the systems being used to manage, forecast, and deal with change are not keeping up.

- Some ways to overcome the barriers to innovation are to empower individuals by providing resources, vision, and an environment that is more comfortable with risk, failure, and experimentation. It requires measuring and incentivizing the right things and making innovation important everywhere in the organization.

- Begin to embrace the uncertainty. Determine how you might use it to focus on what's important or identify what needs to be learned or unlearned. Be thankful for what you have and take action to resolve the tension that uncertainty brings.

QUICK ACTIONS TO DO NOW

Identify three common things that happen to slow down or stifle innovation within your organization. What steps can you take to lower or eliminate these barriers?

1.

2.

3.

Begin to track a variety of innovation metrics to incentivize and encourage innovation. Here's a list of possible metrics to use:

- The number of employees who have received or are receiving innovation-related training

- Employee perception of your organization's innovativeness

- The number of ideas in the innovation pipeline and at what stage

- The time an idea spends in each stage of your innovation pipeline

- The velocity of the ideas through each stage of the pipeline

- The number of new products launched

- Percentage of revenue generated or expenses saved each year from new ideas launched

CHAPTER 4

THE EXPLORATION ENGINE

SEEK AND GATHER

In Chapter 1, we introduced the three engines of innovation needed to navigate the obstacles and opportunities outlined in Chapters 2 and 3. Chapters 4, 5, and 6 will delve into each in more detail, starting with the Exploration Engine.

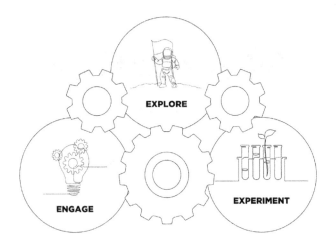

To accelerate innovation, you must find ideas to accelerate. Ideas are the seeds that can grow to create value. Finding new ideas requires exploration. When we explore the new and novel, we expose ourselves to new sources of ideas. In today's rapid environment of change and uncertainty, drawing upon a broader and more accelerated flow of information is needed to keep pace.

Exploration is the process of searching through the

new and unknown to gather inputs and insights. It's the process of learning and unlearning what we know and combining it with the new. Exploration is where ideas can begin to collide, merge, and interact. Psychologist Kevin Dunbar and colleagues estimate that between 30 percent and 50 percent of all scientific discoveries are accidental in some sense. Random collisions of inputs create opportunities for new connections and combinations to emerge. If we are not exposing ourselves to the new and different, innovation does not occur.

Building out your Exploration Engine is all about accelerating this learning process. Because it's impossible to know ahead of time which idea, insight, or knowledge is needed to create the next innovation, it is essential to immerse yourself in a continuous stream of new input. Your innovation efforts will falter without a regular intake of fresh ideas and new insights.

To learn to adapt, you must place yourself in uncomfortable environments that force you to grow. Innovation begins with seeing things differently, asking questions, being curious to learn (and unlearn), and adapting your thinking and actions to a changing, unknown landscape.

The time spent in learning and exploring mode is valuable and leverageable. The right kind of exploration can yield a tenfold return on the time you invest in it. Let's look at the many ways to accelerate your Exploration Engine.

START WITH CURIOSITY

When the world is unknown and uncertain, you must explore to innovate. The easiest way to begin is to explore areas in which you're curious. It starts with a willingness to investigate new subjects, ideas, and areas of knowledge. Seek out information. Read more. Make connections between the new things you're discovering. Become comfortable seeking out new voices. Become a learning machine. Ask questions—lots and lots of questions.

Why is curiosity so critical to innovation? Curiosity instills creativity, promotes collaboration, and is a crucial ingredient to exploration. It's also unlimited and only a question away. When you're curious, you don't have to be perfect. You can be wrong. You can try things and experiment. You can question old maps and determine if they're relevant to the new landscape. Exploring your curiosities kicks off the innovation journey.

SEEK OUT NEW VOICES

Expose yourself to a variety of voices, experiences, and actions. Seek out perspectives, insights, and experiences you don't run into in your everyday routine. Make exploring new voices part of a routine—they give you access to new ideas and knowledge to leverage.

Over the years, I've collected (and now curate) over 500 newsletters, RSS feeds, forums, and other online resources. I spend the first thirty to sixty minutes of each day scanning and reading these new voices and insights with my morning coffee. I imagine this is what my father was doing when he read the morning newspaper daily. Luckily for me (and you), every newspaper, magazine, video, and resource is now available online. I scan these resources for new and interesting things to pique my curiosity. I use this to prime the pump for what's new and next.

I'm constantly adding new voices to the mixes of resources I review. I seek out new podcasts, newsletters, blogs, documentaries, meet-ups, and online groups. I'm a huge advocate for using tools like Twitter or Reddit to identify and follow various streams of conversations.

I began this practice to keep up with new technologies

and trends for my work. I started highlighting and saving interesting stats, articles, images, and other things in Evernote. My various Evernote databases began to fill up with an ever-evolving, searchable resource for me. I later used these curated repositories to share with others. Teams in my NMotion startup accelerator had access to the latest best practices and voices curated daily. Recently I began publishing a series of databases for the InsideOutside.io website and community to use, including databases tracking innovation tools, books, articles, videos, and our *Inside Outside Innovation* podcast guests.

I then began to share what I was finding with friends and colleagues. I created a weekly newsletter focused on talent, technology, and innovation. At first, I did this to keep myself accountable to continue digging into new topics and ideas. I still use this practice today to stay fresh, motivated, and curious. I have amplified the practice by sharing what I find with others. Sharing the resources began to pay other dividends as the audience grew. This daily curation has been a massive help to my cultivation of the curiosity muscle. It has turned into a way to engage new people and voices and to continue building.

The resources I explore and share have changed over

time. It has become a replenishing cycle and habit. It's even provided insight into how my thinking and interests have changed. I can go back chronologically through my notes and scan what I was reading, what I was interested in, and what was trending based on the articles I saved and shared.

A simple way to start curating new voices and inputs is to use the 3-3-3 approach. Choose three sources inside your industry to follow. What are the trade publications, newsletters, and influencer accounts that everyone in your industry pays attention to? Choose another three sources adjacent to your industry and another three outside your sector. Reevaluate and add or change the sources in these three categories each quarter. Over time, you'll develop your go-to resources to access new insights and speed up your learning.

SEEK OUT NEW EXPERIENCES

In addition to new voices, it's essential to seek out new experiences. New experiences and new actions also accelerate and increase your exposure to the inputs for ideas and innovation. Go out and do stuff. Take action to create, build, or try something new, rather than passively learning or reading about it. The simple act of experiencing new things has a dramatically different effect than just reading or learning about them.

Make it a point to push yourself into new activities. Learn firsthand about new people, places, and subjects. New experiences come from doing things we haven't done before, seeing things we haven't noticed, and trying things we haven't tried. Traveling to new places, eating new foods, listening to new music, connecting with new friends, teaching new skills, and building new projects are a few ways to ramp up your experience game. The best way to feed curiosity and the Exploration Engine is to engage with new people, places, and perspectives—exposure to the new and novel is a fertilizer for curiosity.

ASK QUESTIONS

Innovation goes hand in hand with discovery. To execute on innovation, you must reengage with that sense of wonder you had as a child. Instead of assuming something won't work, ask, "What happens if it does work?" or "How might it work?" You must embrace the awkwardness of asking the questions "what if?" and "why not?" Curious people ask questions that start with "how," "what," "when," "where," and "why." Stay away from the yes or no answer and be open to where questions can lead you. Eric Schmidt, the former CEO of Google, said, "We run this company on questions, not answers."

Early on in my career as a consultant, I was often thrown into new markets, industries, and companies with little core knowledge or understanding. The only way to do my job was to ask questions and follow the answers to the next batch of questions. Rinse, repeat.

Sharpening your questioning skills builds your curiosity muscle and accelerates your learning and understanding in unknown environments. Questioning opens you up to more alternatives. The answers lead you to other questions and other options to consider.

I find "what if?" and "why not?" to be some of the best questions to flush out hidden assumptions and barriers, as the answers force reflection on existing held beliefs and practices. By default, these questions challenge the status quo and lead to identifying problems and possible value creation points. Breakthrough discoveries come from asking these breakthrough questions. "What if?" and "why not?" questioning helps prevent confirmation bias, resulting in fewer decision-making errors.

If you do only this, your access to possible innovations will increase significantly. Asking the same questions, walking the same paths, and living in the status quo are no longer options.

One way to get better at asking questions is to explore questions themselves. About once a month, I'll go to Quora. Quora is a website that enables folks to ask questions and crowdsources answers. Readers can upvote favorite answers or add their take on the question. From art to business, you can see what questions people ask and answer. The more questions you review and see how people respond to them, the better you'll get at asking and answering them yourself.

SEEK SURPRISE

Humans crave the comfortable and known. It's self-preserving. But we also have a desire for some surprise. We must seek wonder and embrace the unpredictable and unexpected. That little jolt lets us know we're onto something. Begin to cultivate the move from the comfortable to the unknown.

A quick way to infuse a little jolt of surprise is to pick a new topic each month to explore. Seek wonder in areas like foods you try, places you travel, and people you interact with. Choose a new industry, skill, or historical period to investigate. Take a course in a subject you know nothing about. Read about a historical figure. Learn a new skill. These activities will put you into an environment that will challenge the status quo and give you the variety your innovative mind needs to flourish.

SEEK SERENDIPITY

Look for luck. Christian Busch, author of *The Serendipity Mindset*, talks about the intentional actions to increase the surface area of luck. Be proactive at identifying intersections, patterns, and connections. You can create unexpected opportunities to connect the dots with others. Hang out with interesting people. Join forums and meet-ups where your interests overlap (e.g., art and technology).

One of the best ways I've seen organizations foster innovation is by creating serendipitous opportunities for employees to explore activities in the startup community. Startup events like Startup Weekend, Open Coffee, Accelerator Demo Days, and 1 Million Cups allow employees to interact and learn directly from entrepreneurs. These collisions can accelerate the lessons learned from what it takes to build in unknown and changing environments.

MAKE TIME FOR LEARNING

As you build your curiosity muscle, you should fall into exploration mode more often and at different times. I find it helpful to block time for curiosity endeavors as well. Take intentional pauses to reflect. Block time to think and for random collisions to happen. This exploration time gives you the permission and ability to focus on doing something that might not be immediately valuable. Typically, the nuggets you begin to find during this time become building blocks to more direct value creation later. Set aside 20 percent, one day a week, for learning and exploring. Sneak it into your daily routine. Explore the areas that excite and entertain you. How can these collisions of knowledge and networks begin to give you clarity into the current problems?

One of the ways I block time for curiosity is my weekly Open Coffee meet-up. I started the meet-up in 2012. Every Thursday morning from 8:00–9:00 a.m., I host a table at the same coffee shop (online, during the pandemic) and promote it as a discussion group for innovators and entrepreneurs. One of the best benefits is that it enables me to connect with a growing network of people and carves time to make random connections for me and others.

ANSWER IMPOSSIBLE QUESTIONS

One way to prompt your brain into thinking more creatively is to pose a problem and think through potential ways to get to an answer. We used this at Gartner to think through "impossible" questions. Impossible questions are questions that are difficult to find correct answers for quickly, but you can get close to a solution by thinking creatively about the issue. Questions like, "How many parking spaces are in the United States?" "What industry sold the most microchips during the pandemic?" or "What color is a mirror?"

To answer impossible questions, you must access available information sources and begin building out assumptions to reach a potential, reasonable answer. You must ask yourself what information is required to answer the question and what resources or steps you need to make it happen. You can then begin to triangulate possible answers.

My first assignment as a consultant in Asia in the

mid-nineties was to estimate the size of China's direct-access storage device (DASD) market. I was so new to the area that I had to research what a DASD even was. From there, I began to explore the market players, their distribution channels, and other data points. I interviewed manufacturers, customers, and suppliers and triangulated the data points to find a reasonable answer to the impossible question.

You must think through the problem by first understanding the context. What do I know about who manufactures these devices? How do they sell them? Who buys these products? By thinking through a few of these, I could start planning to gather data points to triangulate an answer. I interviewed vendors in the supply chain and DASD customers to estimate the number and types of devices bought and used. The great thing about this approach is that you can get to a "reasonable" guess and then refine it closer to reality with further interviews, research, and extra time spent on the problem. The more often you ask your brain to flex on these problems, the better and quicker you get.

LIVE IN THE FUTURE

Studying and exploring trends and discoveries opens your connections to what's possible. Take time to imagine the world you're thinking about and creating. Ask the questions, "Wow, that's amazing. What if that actually happened? How is this trend affecting the periphery of what I'm doing now? Can I use any of this knowledge or these insights today?"

I interviewed Ari Popper on episode 80 of the *Inside Outside Innovation* podcast. Ari is the founder of Sci-Futures. SciFutures is a fascinating blend of science fiction and corporate innovation in which sci-fi writers team up with corporations to imagine futures in their industry. Through storytelling, graphic novels, animation, and virtual reality, companies begin to explore the future and open opportunities to create it.

FIND THE PAIN POINTS

One of the best places to find new ideas to accelerate is to look for problems and the people who have them. Talking to customers about their problems is an overlooked and underutilized tactic for finding innovative ideas. When I work with startups or corporate leaders, I encourage them to keep a running list of issues and pain points they run into regularly. Customer conversations and market research focused on discovering pain points are a great way to find ideas that can become innovations.

LEARN TO UNLEARN

The problem for many folks is not learning—it's unlearning. Barry O'Reilly, author of *Unlearn: Let Go of Past Success to Achieve Extraordinary Results*, introduced me to this powerful framework. Barry has been a guest on my podcast and a speaker at our IO Summit. In every aspect of our life, we operate with mental models that have grown outdated. The more success we achieve, the more likely we will fall into the pattern of doing the things that achieved this success in the first place. This works great in an environment with few changes and more certainty. However, when the environment is dynamic, we can't rely on old skills and old maps that no longer deliver the same results.

On the organizational level, models from strategy to marketing to leadership stagnate or become irrelevant in the face of the new and moving landscape of technology and change. What you learned five to twenty years ago in school or work likely no longer applies. Many of the best practices we learned in school are now incomplete or ineffective. To embrace the new ways of value creation, we must unlearn the old ones. Many old models have been built on incremental change, not exponential. When change is exponential, incremental models will not be able to keep pace. As Albert Einstein said, "We cannot solve our problems with the same thinking we used when we created them."

From traditional mass marketing advertising to linear customer journeys, many models are changing. Consumers are now co-creating value. Traditional demographics are less relevant as it becomes harder to place people into discrete buckets of information. Shared experiences are driving engagement, and customer journeys are no longer linear. We see an evolution from formal hierarchies to fluid networks in organizational design. Value creation and competitive advantage change from incremental to exponential in a networked economy. Firms no longer control a single pipe of value creation but instead create a platform and ecosystem of customers, suppliers, and partners. Old models aren't necessarily obsolete, but they are more incomplete given the new and changing landscape. We must unlearn past models or modify and relearn them.

Become an active un-learner. Unlearning does not mean forgetting the old ways; it means being proactive at questioning and looking from the outside to challenge your current thinking and actions. To become an effective un-learner, you must recognize that old mental models are no longer relevant or practical. This can be uncomfortable. Mental models make decisions easier. We have them for a reason. We have built our value on knowing and executing on them. Letting them go can feel like starting over.

Once you check your existing models, you need to form a new mental model to achieve your goals, which can be challenging because you will often see the new model through the lens of the old ones. In the end, innovation is about seeing the world differently and solving practical problems that need to be solved. It starts with developing a culture of learning and unlearning.

WANDER THE CAVE

Every new venture, project, or business can feel like entering a dark cave without a flashlight. To get to the other side, you must enter the cave and explore. Feel your way through. Make some wrong turns. Exit the cave and find another one to try. You can't find the treasure or get to the other side unless you enter and explore the cave. Wandering the cave means acting on your ideas. It means getting out into the real world to test if you are on the right path or if you need to choose a new one. You cannot go from idea to innovation by remaining in the office or conference room guessing what might be inside the cave. Each act of exploring the cave gives you direct information and insights that you can use to move your idea forward.

BEWARE OF OLD MAPS

The more we succeed at something, the more we continue to do the same things that got us there in the first place. This focus can serve you well in stable environments (sports, games, etc.) but becomes challenging in changing settings. What worked yesterday is unlikely to continue to work forever. Living your life under old maps and old assumptions is a recipe for disruption. We must be conscious of old maps solidifying into old habits that don't serve the current environment.

One way to break old habits and old maps is to "flood" or overwhelm the old action with the newly desired action or practice! Complete immersion into a new area can open different ways of thinking and force the old habits and maps out of the way. You need to get comfortable asking yourself if past actions and activities will continue to deliver benefits in the new environment. Instead of thinking about how to be right, be open to being wrong. Questioning your old maps goes a long way to helping you explore new ones.

BECOME A POLYMATH

A great way to accelerate your exploration is by studying a wide range of subjects and topics across various disciplines. People like Bill Gates or Elon Musk are avid polymaths, learning new subjects to then be able to deconstruct ideas into their fundamental principles and then reconstruct them in new ways. Learn like Bill and Elon.

You don't have to sign up for a class at your community college or university anymore, either. A fantastic resource of diverse online educational platforms can give you access to any subject in the world for minimal, if any, cost. Platforms like YouTube, Master-Class, Kahn Academy, Maven, Udemy, and On Deck are changing how you can expand your knowledge and skillset. Better yet, deepen your learning by using your newfound skills to build, prototype, or experiment. Start by making something lame. Most people never even take the step of making something they're embarrassed by. Overcome the fear of starting by embracing being a newbie and not having all the answers. The simple process of creating something can go a long way in your understanding and retention of the subject or skill and begin to build your confidence along the way.

LEARN TO SEARCH

Most problems or ideas are not new. You are not the first to face a particular challenge or explore a specific topic. I encourage innovators to develop a list of resources, databases, and networks they can turn to when exploring new ideas. Who's exploring the same problems, and how are they approaching the situation? The best explorers know this and look for shortcuts. They are masters at understanding that all the world's knowledge is at their fingertips. They know how to use a search engine and navigate resources to find the right information and learn the next thing.

Many new ideas have come from leveraging concepts from other industries or areas of expertise. There's nothing wrong with applying knowledge from somewhere else to a new situation you're facing. Many brilliant innovations have come from stealing ideas from other areas and using them in a different environment.

Henry Ford's car assembly line borrowed innovations

from three industries: interchangeable parts from the watch industry, continuous flow manufacturing from the canning industry, and assembly process from the "disassembly" process of the meatpacking industry. Other examples include BMW, which borrowed concepts for its iDrive navigation systems from the video game industry, and infant incubators, which were inspired by the incubators used in the poultry industry. Don't reinvent the wheel—leverage what's already been explored.

TAKE GOOD NOTES

Gathering new learnings is essential, but leveraging these insights quickly and effectively will give you an edge. One way to do this is to take good notes. There are dozens of note-taking tools out there. Pick one that works for you and use it. I've found that storing interesting articles, notes from conversations, and insights on core topics I'm exploring has enabled me to make connections quicker and leverage new learnings. Each month, I spend time reviewing what I capture, looking for patterns or relationships that I subconsciously collected along the way. Ideas and innovation are rarely linear. Sometimes the spark comes from something you gathered months or years earlier and comes to life when matched with new data or insights. Having a way to organize and review these insights and inspirations can help you act when necessary.

SCHEDULE YOUR SENSES

One of the best ways to build up your muscles of creativity, curiosity, and innovation is to make time to activate different senses each week. Doing so will accelerate collisions with new ideas and expand your connections to new things.

Innovation Accelerators observe patterns and differences. Innovation Accelerators seek the thrill and excitement of seeing something different or trying something new. They make time to activate new senses regularly. They make time to create intersections of ideas, thoughts, and actions.

The trouble is that we get into ruts and routines. Humans crave security and stability. We become numb to the environment, the people, and the ideas we are familiar with. We get comfortable, stagnant. We fall into patterns. We turn to the things we know and the things we already enjoy. Do this for too long, and we end up numb to what's new and limited in our ability to flex the innovation muscles when we need them.

To break from the routine, we must first notice these patterns and then change or enhance them. To form new connections and insights, we must become more observant of the patterns and differences. The simple act of a conscious decision to focus on the new and novel can have profound, cumulative effects. When you focus on the new and novel in one area, you'll start to see the new and novel in other areas as well. These cumulative collisions often lead to new ways of thinking and doing. More importantly, these collisions stack knowledge in a way that enables us to form new pathways or opportunities. New ideas can emerge, and innovations can be created. These new sparks result from hearing or learning about something new and combining that with the information you've accumulated at other times or from other areas.

One method I've used to become more proactive at seeking new and different experiences is something I call "scheduling your senses." This exercise proactively acknowledges and gives you playful permission to get out of your comfort zone and pursue or observe something different. This approach is an intentional nudge from traditional comfort zones to experience ideas and insights in new ways, challenge routines, and open your senses. Scheduling your senses is a way to force your brain to take notice rather than shift into autopilot.

Let's start with the senses. We have five of them to play with: sight, sound, taste, smell, and touch. Scheduling your senses permits you to test new boundaries, try new things, and ask questions about what you are experiencing. The goal of scheduling your senses is to become observant about what you can sense in each situation. What patterns are you experiencing around you? What's different? How can you affect an experience by focusing on or changing something about the situation?

- **Step 1:** Pick a timeframe that you want to "schedule." The timeline can change (hour, day, week, month), but pick a specific start and end time. Choosing a timeframe allows you to focus and challenge your traditional routines. You can also change what you sense and experience by varying the timeframes. One time you may want to focus on a particular sense—what you see, hear, taste, smell, or touch in a short period. Other times you may want to extend the timeframe to allow for more and different types of encounters.

- **Step 2:** Pick a sense you want to schedule: sight,

sound, taste, smell, or touch. You can choose one or combine a few. The key is to be proactive about your area of focus.

- **Step 3:** During the chosen timeframe, observe and take note of the experiences around that sense. What are you noticing? What's different from other experiences, and how does it make you feel? What's the same or different about other experiences? What can you learn from it?

Each week, pick a sense or two to schedule. Each sense will offer many ways to test, try, and experience. The importance is not the specific actions, experiments, or timeline you take but the observations and connections you make. Doing this will make you better at seeing patterns and opening new links when they present themselves. It will help you become more observant and proactive about making and breaking these patterns to open up to new and creative ones.

Even a handful of these activities or exercises will open you to many new ideas, insights, and new opportunities. The more you explore and cultivate your curiosity, the more experiences and reference points you'll have to ideate and iterate when adapting to constant change and uncertainty.

EXPLORATION IN THE ORGANIZATION

Once you begin to build your curiosity muscle and Exploration Engine, you can help others in your organization build theirs. Innovative organizations tend to hire for curiosity, emphasize learning goals, and let employees broaden their exposure and interests. Organizations that can tap into their employees' curiosity show greater overall curiosity, trust, and impact. A recent Harvard study showed that increasing curiosity by one unit led to a 34 percent increase in creativity overall.

Here are some ways to address and encourage an exploration-based organization:

FIND THE CURIOUS AND RESTLESS

At Nelnet, we launched a monthly gathering called Spark. A program we saw in the startup community, 1 Million Cups, was the inspiration. 1 Million Cups was started by the Kauffman Foundation in Kansas City to bring together entrepreneurs and the local community to share and learn. Every Wednesday, over 160 communities meet to give support, encouragement, and feedback to local entrepreneurs over a cup of coffee. The Kauffman program has grown from city to city and exposed a network of entrepreneurs and innovators to each other and other communities.

We modified the gathering at Nelnet to occur monthly within our company but kept the core format. The event starts with fifteen minutes of coffee and networking, followed by a short fifteen-minute presentation. The presentation can be a recap of a recent project, an intro to a new program, a retrospective on a past failure, or a skill-sharing session. We have, on occasion, brought in an outside presenter to share their expertise on a topic outside of Nelnet's core business to expose employees to new thoughts, industries, and ideas.

After the presentations is a fifteen-minute open Q&A session to dig further into their topic. The last question is always, "What can we, as a community, do for you (the speaker)?" This question fuels collaboration and tangible next steps for the speaker and the organization. The final fifteen minutes is more networking and coffee. Each session is recorded and archived. We often point new employees to past Spark sessions to speed up learning and share what is happening across the organization.

We created Spark to identify the curious and restless employees at Nelnet and provide an outlet to share, collaborate, and learn from each other. The purpose of Spark is to expose fellow employees to progress across all divisions. It creates collisions of ideas, people, and resources. Understanding what is happening in other business areas has produced impressive results. It has inspired cross-collaboration on projects, enabled sharing of resources, and sparked new ideas and initiatives.

HIRE FOR CURIOSITY

One of the best ways to build a team of explorers is to hire for curiosity. Look for candidates who demonstrate a variety of interests, hobbies, and side projects. Ask them about activities and interests outside of the job you seek to fill. Have they shown experiences that required exploration to succeed? Do they ask questions and show interest in more than just the job requirements? Don't overlook the cultural misfit.

MODEL INQUISITIVENESS

Leaders and managers need to model curiosity by being inquisitive. Ask the "dumb" questions in front of others. It improves trust and opens up conversations that aren't otherwise available. One technique I've used is to start a meeting going around the room and having folks answer the prompt, "Today, I'm most curious about X," or "I'm wondering about Y."

REWARD LEARNING

Companies often focus purely on performance goals as the primary driver of rewards. Organizations looking to build curiosity should also look at learning goals. They should reward accomplishing objectives around developing competence, acquiring skills, mastering new situations, etc. Recognizing failure not through incompetence but through learning will increase an organization's curiosity chops.

EXPLORE OTHER INTERESTS

Remaining exposed to the same people and environments stifles creativity and innovation. To mitigate this, encourage employees to explore other interests. Look to support side projects inside and outside the organization. At Nelnet, we encourage folks to spend time attending or participating in activities in the startup community.

Most communities have an ecosystem of events available. Startup events like Kauffman's 1 Million Cups, Startup Grind, or local pitch competitions can help employees build networks and connections to new people and ideas. Being a part of events like Startup Weekend can help expose people to new techniques and learn firsthand the speed and skills needed to get new ideas moving forward faster. There are plenty of startup accelerator programs and eager startups looking for mentorship, connections, and collaboration that your team can also tap into. Participating in startup activities can give employees access to new ways of thinking, techniques, and networks that can serve the existing organization.

HOLD "WHAT IF?" DAYS

I've seen success with organizations making time for exploration through events and discussions focused on exploring problems and situations outside the norm. Allowing teams to think past traditional boundaries and constraints can open new opportunities and encourage broader thinking and skill development. "What If?" Days are scheduled practices that permit time for people to explore new skills, tools, or areas of interest that don't always get the attention. Organizations that hold regular "What If?" Days allow teams to dedicate time to pursue activities outside their daily work requirements to explore, build, and try new things that foster a culture of exploration.

QUICK TAKES TO REMEMBER AND SHARE

- To accelerate innovation, you must find ideas to accelerate. Finding new ideas requires exploration inside and outside the organization. The Exploration Engine is where you seek and gather these ideas.

- When the world is unknown and uncertain, you must explore to innovate. Exploration is the process of searching through the new and unknown to gather inputs and insights. Exploration is where ideas can begin to collide, merge, and interact. Building out your Exploration Engine is all about accelerating this learning process.

- Exploration starts with curiosity. It requires us to seek out new voices and experiences and ask questions. Making time for learning, seeking out problems and pain points, and scheduling your senses are skills that can be developed to accelerate your Exploration Engine.

- Once you begin to build your exploration capabilities, you can help others in your organization build theirs. Innovative organizations tend to hire for curiosity, emphasize learning goals, and let employees broaden their exposure and interests.

QUICK ACTIONS TO DO NOW

This chapter outlined several activities you can under-take to kick start your exploration efforts. Pick one and start this week. Sign up for an online class. Curate your 3-3-3 sources for seeking new voices or schedule which sense you want to focus on today. Pick three new subject areas you want to begin to learn more about—one area within your industry, one adjacent to it, and one area completely unrelated.

CHAPTER 5

THE ENGAGEMENT ENGINE

REFLECT AND COLLABORATE

The process of innovation is like putting together a puzzle. If Exploration is where you gather the puzzle pieces, Engagement is where you start to put the pieces together. Engagement is where your ideas collide, mix, and remix. It's where you evaluate, synthesize, and refine your assumptions. Most importantly, it's where you reflect, share, and collaborate with others to sort through and make sense of what's missing and what's not. What new pictures are emerging from what you've learned? What patterns are you noticing? Where are the overlaps? Are there other puzzles you should be looking to solve? Who else can help bring this idea to life?

Your Engagement Engine is where you can tap into resources, talent, and insights to accelerate your ideas to outcomes. You want early feedback and signals on whether you're on the right track and should keep going or you're way off. Is there "something there" with the idea, or do you need to kill it, change it, or shelve it for later?

The Engagement Engine is where you map out your assumptions and begin putting the plans in place to execute and experiment. It's where you engage your ideas to decide what else is needed to explore, refine, test, or experiment.

ENGAGEMENT REQUIRES COLLABORATION

We often think of innovation as a solo endeavor. We default to the lonely scientist toiling away in a lab when *boom*, a spark of inspiration ignites the eureka moment that changes the world. We jump from the initial "invention" past the hard work of implementation and value extraction. We skip over the team and the effort between spark and success. Overnight successes rarely happen overnight.

While the spark or seed of an idea often comes from an individual, value creation rarely happens in a vacuum, especially in today's environment. We often overlook the collaborative and team nature of innovation. It takes an ecosystem to build a startup idea, nurture it, experiment, learn, grow, and scale it.

And while you can put together a puzzle all by yourself, the fastest way to accelerate progress is to engage others in the process. We likely have access to the answers and the help needed, but it's often siloed or left untapped. How do you tap into the collective intelligence of your organization and network? How do we engage with others to strengthen and grow our ideas into things of value? Accelerating your Engagement Engine requires you to build a network of advocates, mentors, teammates, and go-to resources.

You need a diverse network to give you access to new insights, learnings, and new talent to partner with and insulate you from sudden changes and challenges. Likewise, an organization needs to foster a more comprehensive network of collaborators to help bring innovation to light. You need a network that can change as you grow and learn.

The rapid pace of change is ushering in an era of mass collaboration with the best innovators amassing the best and brightest talent network. Your network is crucial for navigating exponential change. Your network is a core component that will affect your success or failure.

MAP YOUR NETWORK

An excellent way to accelerate your Engagement Engine is to understand your collaborative network. When looking to fast-track engagement in your ideas, it's good to have various groups and perspectives from which to draw. No one person is intelligent enough or skilled enough in today's environment to go it alone. You need a combination of generalists and specialists at your disposal.

The good news is that all the world's knowledge and

connections are likely in your pocket right now. In 2010, roughly 25 percent of the world's population was connected to the internet. Over the next decade, the convergence of broadband, 5G, and satellite networks brought 1 billion new people online, creating the largest interconnected innovation lab in history. By 2021, internet penetration reached 4.7 billion people—60 percent of the world. Over the next decade, the rest of humanity will join the conversation, networked together at gigabit speeds.

Talent is now everywhere and more accessible than ever. Your network can now have the capability to tap into experts no matter where they live. Now's the time to access the collective intelligence of your network. Map yours out. Who do you have in your network who can help, and who do you need to meet?

Start by listing your primary contacts who might be able to contribute to the idea(s) you're exploring—those go-to people you might engage for advice and feedback on the specific topic of interest. These folks can be mentors, colleagues, friends, family, or known experts. Connect the dots with people in your network from the media you consume (blogs, podcasts, Twitter) to the places you go (conferences, webinars, travel) to the places you hang out (industry groups, local activities, social forums). Don't forget to map your network outside your organization. Your outside network serves as a radar for change and should bring you different perspectives, ideas, and opportunities. Your external network will enable you to learn and execute faster.

Take stock of the list. How did you meet those in your network? Who's missing? Examine the list's diversity. Is everyone from the same city? industry? social circles? Look for "super connectors"—the people in your network who can introduce you to other people and networks beyond your immediate contacts. Is there anyone on the list who would be able to challenge or provide contrarian thoughts on the topic?

This simple exercise will help you uncover gaps or opportunities to expand and use other networks when required. You should look to cultivate various groups, sub-groups, or clusters of contacts that can add value and to which you can do the same.

I tap into many collaborative networks, depending on location, time, industry, or interest topics. These networks build and grow in value over time. My friends and contacts I made when working in Asia have now spread around the globe and work in various industries, locations, and positions. The founders, investors, and community leaders I met while building NMotion and the Midwest startup ecosystem have been invaluable in accelerating nearly every idea and innovation I've tried in the past decade. I have a cluster of colleagues at Nelnet that enables me to navigate and add value across a large organization.

I take part in and engage with various groups to help me inform and act on my ideas. Some of the groups I lean on include startup founders, investors, corporate innovators, past and present customers, no-code builders, creators, artists, friends, and coworkers from other countries or industries, hobby groups, and the list goes on.

Polish your LinkedIn profile and be open to connecting. Share your new projects or learnings with online communities and associations. Reach out for help. I like interacting with new founders and builders at Product Hunt and through AngelList. Some of my best friends and colleagues have come from a simple question or outreach via Twitter.

We are entering an era of mass collaboration. Talent and expertise are everywhere. The best innovators are amassing a diverse network of talent both inside and outside their organizations. What are the relationships in your organization that you need to nurture and grow? Who are the experts in your field that you want to learn from?

You need this diverse network to access new insights and talent with which to partner. The diversity of your network can insulate you from sudden changes and challenges and open you up to unexpected opportunities.

Networks are powerful because they can accelerate all aspects of moving an idea to an outcome. They can help speed up the learning process, address assumptions and challenges, and help amplify adoption. Your network can provide access to information, talent, and resources. To navigate an accelerating world, cultivate and build your network.

GROW YOUR NETWORK

Once you've mapped out your network, look for ways to expand or fill in the gaps to increase value. The simplest way to do this is to look for ways to grow your network by sharing your knowledge, expertise, and network with others. Brad Feld, the author of *Startup Communities* and partner at Foundry Group, talks about the power of a "give first" mindset. Your default response in most situations should be to ask how you can add value without the need for a direct or immediate transaction in return. If you approach network building with this mindset, your network will grow in size and impact. Help others accelerate their ideas, and more often than not, you will have a network that will reciprocate the favor when you need help.

You can also grow your network by cultivating reasons for clusters in your network to connect. Host events and meet-ups, and mastermind dinners. Start a project and ask for folks to contribute. Do the inviting and handpick the folks you can help and who can help you. These proactive collisions can go a long way in fostering a strong network for short- or long-term success.

To maximize your chances of learning things you don't know already, mobilize the weak ties in your network. Weak ties are the relationships you have with people you don't know so well or don't see very often. These cross-cluster interactions sometimes offer the most insight or a fresh set of eyes on a problem.

Cultivate your immediate team. Make sure you have

the right mix of cross-functionality. A diverse team with a variety of talents can learn and iterate faster. You can divide and conquer and tap into their networks as well, for advice, insights, and resources. Your immediate team can also consist of your suppliers, partners, and competitors inside and outside your industry.

Finally, don't forget to tap into your customers and early adopters. One of the best ways to accelerate your ideas is engaging with customers. Look for ways to build solutions together that can offer rapid, real-life feedback.

ENGAGE CUSTOMERS

Your customers are some of the most overlooked and undervalued people in your network. One of the most effective ways to accelerate your ideas is to engage with customers early and often in the innovation process. Understanding and engaging with customers can offer rapid, real-life feedback and enable you to build solutions together.

Customer discovery is the process of understanding customers' needs, situations, and pain points. It is the first of the four stages of the customer development process pioneered by Steve Blank, author of *The Four Steps to the Epiphany* and *The Startup Owner's Manual*, and a person I had the pleasure of interviewing on episode 216 of the *Inside Outside Innovation* podcast. Steve outlined the process that helps you test your assumptions about your business using direct feedback from customers.

Customer discovery starts with understanding a customer's pain points. The number one reason most ideas fail is that the pain point isn't big enough to be an attractive opportunity. If the problem is not big enough, strong enough, or frequent enough, it is usually a signal to keep exploring. When you develop a solution without validating a need or understanding the customer's buying process, journey, and barriers, you are setting your idea up to fail. Every hour spent on customer discovery saves hours writing, coding, designing, or guessing what needs to be developed and delivered.

One of the best ways to engage customers is to conduct customer discovery interviews. A lot has been written about the customer discovery process and how to do it effectively. At NMotion, customer discovery was a core component of the program we helped startups undertake. The lessons learned have carried over to working with many corporate product teams as well. Here are some of the things I've learned along the way:

- Since customer needs and circumstances constantly change, you should treat customer discovery as an ongoing, iterative process. When you build customer discovery into your innovation culture, you will see long-term effects in your ability to quickly determine which ideas to pursue, pivot, or place on hold.

- Whether you're a startup with no customers or an existing enterprise with millions, it's best to start the customer discovery process assuming you know nothing about the customer's life or how they're doing their job. Using a "start from scratch" approach allows you to explore with fresh eyes to find relevant things you wouldn't have thought to ask about or explore. It lets you map a more detailed and complete picture of how the customer thinks and acts on your study topic. I've seen this approach lead a startup to a complete pivot. Engaging early customers led the startup to a more pressing problem that was easier to solve and more significant in scale. If the startup hadn't taken this broader approach, it might have limited its outcomes and opportunities.

- Talk about problems, not solutions. People love talking about problems. Indulge them. Listen to where their answers take you. When you introduce solutions into the conversation, it can become too sales focused. This can distract, derail, or bias reactions.

- Don't ask customers what they will do in the future. People are terrible at predicting their future actions. Most of the time, a customer can't answer the question, or they give answers they think you want to hear. Instead of forward-looking or future-based questions, ask them to describe past behaviors and incidents around the topic you're exploring. Not only will you get more accurate feedback, but you'll also likely get more emotional responses that can indicate whether you're on the right path.

- Get excited to hear things you don't want to hear. Don't be discouraged when you run into an answer that's not what you hoped for. Every assumption you disprove helps minimize the waste of time, money, and resources spent building or delivering something the customer doesn't want.

- Plan questions around what you are trying to learn and what you'll do with the information if you're right or wrong. Go into each customer discovery session asking yourself, "What are the decisions we need to make based on what we find out?"

- Use open-ended questions. One-word answers rarely provide details and insights. If you must use an occasional yes or no question, follow it with a "Why?" or "Tell me more about that."

- Always end the interview by asking for referrals for others to talk to. This approach makes it easier to find interview candidates and signals the intensity of the problem.

- Take notes and record the interviews when possible. After completing the interview, summarize it, and add additional details. You'll want good notes to look for patterns and apply actions later. I've seen good notes referred to repeatedly for future customer discovery interviews, during product development, and as references for specific words to use in marketing campaigns months later.

- Interview customers until you see consistent patterns. You're probably onto something if you begin to hear the same answers. You can typically find what you need with fewer than thirty to forty interviews. You will usually see patterns in as few as five to ten discussions. If nothing seems consistent, you're probably interviewing different customer segments, or there's no standard or underlying issue to address.

- Host an ongoing customer advisory board. A customer advisory board is a collection of customers who gather regularly to lend insights to the product development process. A customer advisory board can provide ongoing feedback, ask challenging questions, and provide valuable insights into what customers think, feel, and do.

SAMPLE CUSTOMER DISCOVERY QUESTIONS

- Tell me about the last time you did XYZ.

- What was challenging/difficult about it?

- What did you do yesterday? Tell me about how that went.

- Were there any problems? What do you do next?

- Tell me about the last time you thought, "There's got to be a better way to do this."

- Tell me about all the problems you have related to XYZ?

- What is working well with XYZ?

- Tell me about the last time you had an outstanding experience.

- What part of the XYZ process was the most difficult? Which part required the least effort?

- If you could wave a magic wand and change one thing about how you're doing XYZ today, what would it be?

- What do you wish you could do right now that you can't?

- Have you ever paid for XYZ?

THE POWER OF LANGUAGE

If the Engagement Engine is the place to share your ideas and what you're learning to inform what to do next, it's crucial to understand how to share your ideas and the language you can use to get the most favorable outcomes.

One of the worst things you can do to get honest feedback on your idea is to ask, "What do you think of my idea?" It's like asking, "What do you think of my baby?" Generally speaking, people don't want to hurt your feelings, so they will lie to protect you. Or they give you caveats that may or may not reflect their actual behaviors.

The less you can do to make the feedback personal, the more likely you'll get honest feedback. Pretend it's not your idea. Distance yourself from it. Pretend you don't think it's a good idea. Make it known that it's one of many ideas you're considering. Don't tell them how hard you've been working on the idea, how much you love it, or how you have no other options you're considering. If possible, try to observe people interacting with the concept "in the wild." What are the actual behaviors you're seeing? All these will help when sharing your ideas for engagement.

The other key area of engagement is the language you use when discussing ideas and innovation. My dad was an English professor, so I was taught from an early age the importance of words. Words have influence and impact and can bring clarity. The words we use to describe our ideas can significantly impact the results we get. The language we use can open up discoveries or cut them down before they take off. If we want to accelerate our idea engagement, we need to pay attention to our words.

I learned more of this from Jack Elkins, Founder of Sidekick Innovation and former Director of Innovation for the NBA's Orlando Magic. Jack was instrumental in developing the Magic's innovation lab and spoke at our Inside Outside Innovation Summit about how the Magic used language to teach and sustain innovation.

Here are a few phrases, words, and questions used to reframe and engage ideas:

- "We can, if..." This phrase helps people look for answers and possibilities before talking about barriers and inhibitors.

- Use "yes, and" not "yes, but." An old improv tool

is to expand the scene and the opportunities by using "yes, and..." rather than "yes, but..." language. This simple substitution opens doors rather than closing them.

- "How Fascinating!" "How Cool!" Great phrases to help people suspend or defer judgment during moments of ambiguity, mistakes, or fear. These phrases also enable folks to praise action over highlighting errors.

- "What else?" "Tell me more!" "Why?" These words foster the seeking of deeper understanding and encourage learning.

- "That makes me think of..." This phrase helps build off other experiences and enables people to explore new connections.

- "We don't know how to do it...yet!" This expression orients the conversation with a growth mindset rather than a fixed mindset. It enables further exploration and ideas.

- "How might we accomplish X despite Y?" This question helps teams start with more divergent thinking, opening up more possibilities. It also calls out the assumed constraints to explore further.

- "What I like about that..." A positive way to start an evaluation or judgment without losing creative momentum.

- "I'd like to propose an experiment." Framing a project or action as an experiment lowers the perceived risks and fears and gives permission to explore further. It also serves to define the next steps or actions to continue learning.

- "Thank you." One of the most overlooked phrases during times of stress and uncertainty is "thank you." Having a grateful attitude and respect for the process enables better feedback, integration, and collaboration.

I've found that incorporating these phrases and similar language has led to better group dynamics and a more consistent focus on the positive aspects of innovation culture. Use them as you engage, reflect, and collaborate on your ideas as you move them along.

Engaging ideas and navigating change is a team sport.

Build out your team, show your love, give first, add value, then watch your opportunities expand.

QUICK TAKES TO REMEMBER AND SHARE

- The Engagement Engine is where your ideas collide, mix, and remix. It's where you evaluate, synthesize, and refine your assumptions. Most importantly, it's where you reflect, share, and collaborate with others to put the plans in place to execute and experiment.

- Accelerating your engagement requires you to build a network of advocates, mentors, teammates, and go-to resources. You need a diverse network to give you access to new insights, learnings, and talent to partner with and insulate you from sudden changes and challenges.

- One of the most effective ways to accelerate your ideas is to engage with customers early and often in the innovation process. Understanding and engaging with customers can offer rapid, real-life feedback and enable you to build solutions together.

- To accelerate your idea engagement, pay attention to the words and language used. Be positive, open, and inviting to feedback.

QUICK ACTIONS TO DO NOW

The Engagement Engine brings others along with you to accelerate your ideas to create valuable outcomes. Undertake one of the activities outlined in this chapter, such as mapping out your network, or start by making a list of three people you can reach out to this week to help you explore a particular idea you're working on. Better yet, target three customers and do some customer discovery.

CHAPTER 6

THE EXPERIMENTATION ENGINE

ACT AND EXAMINE

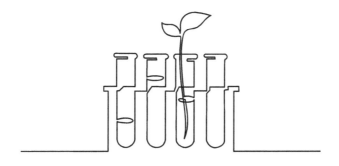

The third engine of innovation is the Experimentation Engine. None of the work spent exploring and engaging ideas matters unless you take action to test, try, and transform your ideas into something of value. Once you seek and gather ideas, reflect, and collaborate on them, it's time to act. This chapter will walk you through a process to help teams quickly move ideas forward faster.

Most ideas begin as a messy bundle of untested assumptions. At these earliest stages, all ideas begin as startups, searching for a model that can be repeatable, scalable, and eventually optimized. Experimentation allows us to manage this uncertainty and risk. The goal should be rapid learning and discovery to search for a model that works before the resources run out. A good innovation process takes a new idea and de-risks the assumptions along the way. Removing this uncertainty and risk creates value.

In this startup phase, it is virtually impossible to pick the outlier winners. If we knew which ideas would work, we'd choose the good ones, execute a plan, and reap the rewards. Unfortunately, there are too many variables between an initial idea and successful implementation to do this.

Even the best venture capital companies, whose core job is to pick winning innovations, do so at a low rate. The common rule in startup investing is that if you invest in ten startups, three or four will fail completely. Another three or four return the original investment, and one or two will produce substantial returns. A top-tier VC firm in Silicon Valley will see approximately 3,000–4,000 startups looking for venture funding in any given year. They will evaluate 200 and fund twenty. In total, the top VCs fund about 200 startups per year. Assuming 200 get funded, only fifteen of those startups will generate all the economic returns. You must invest in far more ideas to achieve outsized results.

Since a large percentage of new ideas typically fail, you must accelerate the number of trial ideas. The key to capturing value at this stage is placing many smaller bets that de-risk new models as they develop. To invest in more ideas, you must accelerate their transformation. You need to get better at killing or pivoting ideas that aren't showing promise and picking new ones to fill the funnel in their place. Let's take a deeper dive into what it takes to act on an idea to move it forward.

ADOPT A SIDE PROJECT MINDSET

To accelerate ideas, you must first get out of your own way. What holds people back from launching their ideas? All too often, people fear looking stupid or being wrong. Ideas at the early stages can look unimpressive, even to their creators. To move ideas forward, you must get out of the mindset that an idea must be perfect at inception. There's a tendency to put too much pressure on early ideas to be fully formed and executable.

Execution of an idea rarely goes as initially planned. Therefore, it's best to treat ideas as guesses or hypotheses to be validated. You can then build experiments and test assumptions. You can kill, pivot, or shelve ideas based on what you discover. You can eliminate the fear of being perfect or needing to have all the answers up front. You can remain objective because an idea's success is based on evidence and progress, not subjective hunches or political winds.

The best way I've found to do this is to treat early-stage ideas as "side projects." Adopting a side project mindset lowers expectations, provides air cover for mistakes, and allows greater experimentation when figuring things out. Many ideas that grow to become scalable business models start with a "side project" mindset. Positioning early-stage ideas and innovations as side projects can take the pressure off finding immediate results in a yet undefined environment. Trying to force early innovation efforts into an existing business environment will kill it. Placing a "side project" label on it can give a project space in the messy learning and exploration phase.

Some of the most significant opportunities in my career have grown from a side project effort. The entire InsideOutside.io community grew out of a side project we created when running the NMotion startup accelerator. In 2014, while running the accelerator, investing in startups, and building a network for Midwest entrepreneurs, we had the idea to try spinning up a weekly podcast to tell the stories of startups and provide an inside look at startups outside Silicon Valley.

The side project grew and changed as we iterated with format and style. We learned from our audience and adapted. After the first year, we launched the second podcast, *Inside Outside Innovation*, which focused on corporate innovators. We were getting asked by more prominent companies about the rise of startups and the tools and methods we talked about to help our startups grow and scale so fast. The ideas and tactics that we were assisting startups to learn and explore, such as lean startup, customer discovery, and iterative experimentation, resonated with larger companies trying to adapt and grow.

Our podcast experiment led us to develop small meet-up events and eventually create the annual Inside Outside Innovation Summit. The IO Summit brings together our podcast audience, corporate innovators, startups, and new converts to the ideas presented in this book and elsewhere.

What started as a simple experiment to test an up-and-coming media format has grown into a thriving consulting, coaching, media, and event business. What began as a side project has grown into a successful platform and network that links hundreds of startups to connections, capital, and resources, teaching corporate innovators and linking communities of innovators together across the Midwest and elsewhere.

We continue to use the "side project" mindset and methodology to launch and try new ideas to grow, such as expanding into helping innovators connect with the latest "no-code" movement. This book started as a side project to capture and share what we have learned and taught over the years.

UNDERSTAND WHY IDEAS FAIL

For an idea to grow and scale, it must have these three elements: desirability, feasibility, and viability. All must be present for an idea to take off. This trifecta has become a cornerstone of work from IDEO in the '70s through practitioners of various inputs to the lean startup, customer discovery, and business model canvas movements. Many of these individuals have become my friends and mentors, including David Bland, Janice Fraser, Tristan Kromer, Jeff Gothelf, Josh Seiden, Justin Wilcox, Tendayi Viki, Barry O'Reilly, Ben Yoskovitz, Alistair Croll, Diana Kander, Alex Osterwalder, and many more.

First, let's look at desirability. For an idea to become valuable, it must be desirable. Does anybody care? Does anyone want to pay in some way to have the problem solved? Is there a big enough pain point to do anything about it? There must be a need, want, or core desire for the idea to get traction.

Second, the idea must be feasible. Can we do it? Feasibility means there's an ability to develop a solution with the right skills, knowledge, and capabilities. Notwithstanding the laws of physics, there are usually ways to solve problems with enough time, money, resources, and effort. Questions you can ask: Can the problem be solved? Do we have the capabilities and team to solve this problem?

The third element of a valuable idea is viability. Should we do it? If an idea is desired and feasible to solve, can you do it profitably in the long term, and are we the right ones to make it happen? Does it align with business goals? Is it worth us trying to solve it? Viability aspects of whether an idea will work also come down to the strategic decision of whether you should solve it.

Ideas can fail if they miss any one of these elements, but the essential one is usually desirability. New ideas typically fail because of a lack of desirability— the problem is not big enough, painful enough, or as widespread as thought. Too many technologies and solutions are built first and then try to find a customer group or market with that problem. The challenge is that after a solution has been created, it's harder to adapt it or change it to meet the actual customer requirements or needs. Too many folks try to wedge the solution into that market, requiring rework, lost resources, lost time, and often lost opportunities. Sometimes an idea works with minimal desirability (or works a little bit), but usually it doesn't.

Ideas rarely fail due to someone not being able to determine a way to solve the problem. After all, we've taken people to the moon. Within the laws of physics, we can solve most problems with enough time, resources, and effort. The same goes for viability. An idea's chance for success goes way up if you can find a group that truly desires it. One can more likely find a viable way to make an idea work if there is a big enough pain point that people are willing to pay for the problem to be solved.

How these three elements work together can impact success or failure. A problem may be desirable to only a small group of people, making it too unprofitable a niche to be viable. A problem may be desirable and viable but not feasible if you don't have the tools or team to solve it. Alternatively, you may be able to feasibly solve a problem, but not at a profit point that makes it worth the effort, thus failing the viability criterion. All three criteria interact with each other.

An Innovation Accelerator's job is to develop the skills and methodologies to test and refine solutions to find the sweet spot of desirability, feasibility, and viability for new ideas and innovations to take off. Here are some ways we've learned to navigate the elements to find attractive market solutions to new ideas and innovations.

BECOME CUSTOMER OBSESSED

To accelerate your ideas, become customer obsessed. Customer-centric leaders focus on the questions like:

- What pain points are customers experiencing and why?

- How do customers work or solve these problems today?

- How do I make their life better?

- What would it take to get them to try or buy?

- How much money and time would I save them?

- How do I make them a hero?

PROBLEMS BEFORE SOLUTIONS

Innovation is all about the creation of value. To create value, you have to solve problems that people find valuable. How do you identify problems to solve? Ask! Everyone can tell you their problems. That's the great part about starting an innovation journey with them. People love to talk about their issues. Just ask or observe. Where's the pain? How often does it happen?

Who has the pain? Who is paying to solve the problem? Is it big? Is it worth solving? Can it be solved? For big problems, is there a chance to make a tenfold impact in the world if solved?

One of the biggest mistakes I've seen from startups and corporate innovators alike is beginning the innovation journey focused on the solution and not the problem. When you start with a solution, you start with the inherent boundaries and limitations of the solution itself. You see the problem through what the solution can do rather than what the problem holder may or may not want solved. People can get enamored with solutions. The potential of new features and the sexiness of building can sometimes cause companies to overlook actual market needs and problems. With over three hundred thousand patents filed in the US annually, patent offices are filled with inventions and solutions yearning for someone to need, use, or want them.

LOOK FOR SHARK BITE PROBLEMS

Not all problems are created equal. If you get an insect bite, you may address the problem with a Band-Aid or ointment. Most folks just live with the situation because it usually goes away with time. The problem isn't big enough to take action.

But what if the bite were bigger? Like a shark bite. Your reaction and effort to address the problem would be significantly different. Shark bite problems require immediate assistance. Chances are you'd be willing to do almost anything to address it. You'd scream for help. You'd try things you've never tried before. You'd pay anything to get to a hospital.

Every market has insect bite problems and shark bite problems. Insect bite problems are simpler to solve but may not be worth solving in the first place. Shark bite problems are severe. They are more challenging and costly to deal with, but they happen far less than insect bites. It helps to know what type of problem you are working with. The type of problem can help you determine the desirability of the problem. Who's trying to solve it? How hard are they trying to solve it?

Knowing the type of problem can help you better understand the solution you need to develop. That impacts on the feasibility of the solution. More complex issues are harder to solve, making them more costly or challenging, affecting the viability or feasibility of a solution. However, people facing shark bite problems are more willing to tolerate less-than-optimal solutions or pay more to address the problem.

The challenge comes when you don't know the type of problem you are dealing with—when you think you are solving a shark bite problem but find out that it is not severe enough. Humans aren't always rational. It happens. Sometimes the timing isn't right. Sometimes the person isn't educated enough about the problem, and the time and effort needed to get them to that point aren't worth the effort. When you apply an expensive shark bite solution to an insect bite problem, your actions can become misaligned. Misalignment requires time and resources to recover from—time and resources you don't always have.

NICHE THEN GROW

One of the best ways to find early traction is to focus on the problem of a single group of early adopters. These are the ones struggling, raising their hands, or otherwise requesting help in solving the problem. We often think that a problem isn't valuable to solve unless we see a massive market or tons of people struggling. The reality is that huge markets start small. Outside the vaccine for a pandemic, most problem sets grow with a few folks who encounter the problem and see it as a big pain point. Those folks may be trying stuff on their own, duct-taping their solutions together, telling their friends, or sharing with other early adopters.

These early adopters could also be tinkerers who like to delve into new and different problem sets.

By finding and focusing on a niche, an entrepreneur or innovator can find a group willing to put up with the solution-building process and work iteratively to solve the problem. They then become advocates and mouthpieces to convince the early majority of people to give it a try. Eventually, as Geoffrey Moore laid out in his book *Crossing the Chasm*, the solution may jump the chasm from early adopters to find a larger majority market.

Think of a great product or company today. They all started with a niche audience of early adopters who typically had more significant pain points and worked with them to grow the market. Facebook started as a social experiment to connect Harvard students. As Mark Zuckerberg grew and iterated on the solution, he expanded to the niche of the Ivy League schools, then colleges in general, before crossing to a mainstream "everyone on the planet" market. If he had tried to build a solution for everyone from the beginning, he would have missed out on all the learnings of a concentrated few.

The solution would likely have been too broad and be

unappealing to everyone. Uber started with the niche of the black-car-service market before taking on all taxi and transportation markets. The iPhone launched with a niche of new features to a limited audience on AT&T's platform. Tesla first sold expensive, high-end Roadsters and used its learnings in this niche to grow to build its Model S luxury sedans. Eventually, it developed the lower-cost, premium Model 3 sedan, which grew to outsell BMW, Mercedes, Audi, and Lexus.

THE 1-2-3-4 PROCESS

Since it's nearly impossible to pick winners at the onset of an idea, you must have a process to let winners develop. To do this, you need to place many small bets, doubling down on the ones that show evidence, traction, or growth and retiring those that don't.

I developed a process to help teams accelerate early-stage ideas called 1-2-3-4. The 1-2-3-4 process is a collection of activities and stage gates or decision points. During each stage, the idea gathers feedback and evidence that the opportunity is still worth pursuing. As the idea proceeds, it is de-risked at each stage. Teams and ideas that show progress and evidence are allocated more time and resources as an idea is de-risked and built out at each stage.

The 1-2-3-4 process is a way to vet ideas while minimizing the risks and resources deployed along the way. It provides a way to research, test, experiment, and move ideas down the path—either killing those that aren't working or doubling down on those that show evidence, traction, and growth.

Idea Generation & Feedback

Idea Brief & Assumption Modeling

Validation & Experiments

1 Minute

2 Hours
$

3 Days
$$

4 Weeks
$$$

Each number in the process represents a time box: 1 minute, 2 hours, 3 days, and 4 weeks. Breaking the idea transformation process into these steps provides a set amount of time to focus on the idea and progress. The end of each step is a decision point to determine if the concept should move on to the next investment stage.

Additional resources are allocated at each stage, increasing as the idea shows traction. The process is similar to allocating resources in startup investing, with incremental and increasing investments made as the idea grows and is de-risked in the market. The process provides a cadence to escalate the investment in time, money, and resources spent at each stage, based on de-risking the idea along the path. If the evidence shows compelling reasons to continue at each stage, then the idea proceeds. If not, the idea is shelved, pivoted, or killed, and a new one is added to begin the journey again. A team finding out early that an idea is not worth pursuing is a win because resources that would have been deployed to a failing or stalled idea can be reallocated.

These metered, incremental bets allow teams to grow, pivot, or kill an idea at each stage based on facts and evidence gathered during discovery and execution in the marketplace. It enables teams to "fail fast" and to progress (or not) based on market feedback and execution.

The 1-2-3-4 process offers several things:

- Provides an approach to act on an idea, get feedback, and begin moving it forward (or not).

- Takes away the pressure of needing "perfect" ideas.

The default state of the process is to assume that all ideas will have flaws and misassumptions. Our guesses will likely be wrong in some areas. The goal is to find evidence and insight to refine the idea and improve it at each step. Making the default state, "This is probably a bad idea," eliminates the pressure to be right at the beginning of the journey when possible answers and assumptions are unknown.

- Allows ideas and projects to be killed or shelved faster so that you can deploy resources into the ideas and projects that show evidence of traction and positive movement. Most companies allow too many zombie projects to continue, sucking resources rather than killing the idea and reapplying resources to other projects showing evidence of working.

- Minimizes political or subjective feedback. Ideas are evaluated based on evidence and feedback from the market, not the whims or assumptions of management or others.

- Enables individuals and teams to receive or allocate resources if an idea meets the criteria to continue and be accountable for the tasks and outcomes of moving it forward.

- Right-sizes the timelines. Anything that takes a month can be done in a couple of weeks, days, or hours, to varying degrees of effectiveness and certainty. Ask yourself what level of learning, clarity, and insights you would get if you had only two hours to find an answer. What could you research? Who could you ask? Start there and work your way up the timeline. Sometimes it will take weeks or months to de-risk an assumption, and that's okay. But sometimes, a quick conversation will get you an answer to continue to the next experiment.

A formalized innovation process can help explore the sea of ideas, problems, and opportunities to find the ones that should be invested in further. This can empower everyone to be a part of the process and encourage the right time and resource investments at each stage. The process helps maintain transparency around company priorities to keep everyone aligned and enables individuals to challenge those ideas objectively. Throughout the process, teams should ask and answer the questions, "What do I need to learn next to prove that we are on the right path to growing the opportunity, and what experiments/actions do I need to take to learn this?"

Here's a summary of the initial stages of investment and inquiry:

1 MINUTE: CAPTURE THE IDEA

Ideas must come from somewhere. An innovation engine only works when people feed it with ideas. The first step in the innovation process is to capture the initial seed of an idea. It's that ah-ha moment, that observation of a problem, or that brief combination of insights that makes you think you're onto something. During this phase, your job is to take note of the idea—what happened, what the insight was, who was involved, etc. Capture the idea. The 1-minute phase provides a starting point for an unvetted idea to simmer, percolate, or collide with other ideas and insights.

2 HOURS: INITIAL FEEDBACK

An idea moves to the 2-hour stage when you have evidence that the idea is worth a 2-hour investment (think long lunch) to further flesh out the concept and circulate it around for some initial feedback. During the 2-hour stage, you are encouraged to submit innovation opportunities by completing an idea brief. The idea brief is a one- to two-page document that outlines the proposed idea and the initial assumptions about the customer, problem, and opportunity to evaluate. The document should not be considered a finalized execution plan but the first stake in the ground about the problem and opportunity. Many of the answers may be "I don't know yet."

Creating the idea brief and the document's sharing for feedback forms the initial "2-hour" bet. In this stage, the problem and opportunity are outlined and presented for feedback. The 2-hour stage aims to showcase the initial assumptions about the opportunity and gather support to pursue the idea further. At the end of the 2-hour bet, the idea can be killed, shelved to explore later, or green-lit and moved to the 3-day stage.

The idea brief is not meant to be perfect, and many of the answers may not be known at the onset. Many of the answers will be assumptions that need to be validated. The brief aims to outline on paper as many thoughts and insights as possible and use them to solicit feedback about what's on track and what's missing.

The idea brief should attempt to answer and provide insights into the following:

- An elevator pitch to describe the opportunity in 240 characters or less. A short and sweet statement to get attention and start the conversation.

- Problem statement: What is the problem you are proposing to solve? Who has it? How often does it occur? How painful is the problem compared to other priorities?

- Is the problem large, urgent, and valuable? If you only have one criterion, it's likely not an idea to pursue immediately. Two out of three is a good start. Have all three, and you have a potential blockbuster.

- Customer segment(s): Who has the problem? Demographics, psychographics, etc.? Who are other influencers and stakeholders?

- Market opportunity: Possible size of the market, competitive landscape, leverage points, or special differentiators within the company.

- Potential team and resources required for the next phase or level of learning. In the early 1-2-3-4 process, it is almost always only one or two people. A larger, cross-functional team may be required by the time an idea moves to the 4-week stage and beyond.

- Unique insight or special sauce: Why is your team interested in tackling this idea? What special skills, background, talent, or insights do you bring to the project?

- Business model canvas (BMC): I recommend using Strategyzer's business model canvas to visually map out the initial assumptions and model to be explored. The BMC can be completed or further developed after an idea proceeds through each phase.

During the initial 2-hour stage, we realize that many of these answers in the idea brief will be unproven assumptions that need to be researched, validated, and addressed. Still, it provides the initial baseline for exploring and pursuing (until market evidence tells us otherwise).

In addition to completing the idea brief document, the 2-hour stage is the time to share the idea and get initial feedback by talking to peers, customers, or industry experts. Use Google and your network to research the current landscape for the concept. Identify any evidence that you might be onto something and incorporate this into the idea brief.

Once completed, the idea brief can be presented to a manager or decision board to evaluate and seek further resources. A person can also continue to research or validate the idea independently as a continued side project. The goal is to assess which ideas have some initial evidence that would make them worth deploying additional time, money, or resources to move the concept to the 3-day stage.

3 DAYS: MODEL HYPOTHESIS AND MAP ASSUMPTIONS

Once a 2-hour idea has the go-ahead to proceed, it enters the 3-day stage (think long weekend). The 3-day stage is when the initial idea assumptions are further researched and developed over a short 3-day sprint. The idea brief is further developed during this stage, and a more detailed business model canvas is created. The business model canvas outlines the yet unproven model for generating value and the initial assumptions for creating and delivering value. The 3-day sprint will outline the riskiest assumptions that need to be validated, along with a plan for what needs to be learned next and the experiments or research required to learn it.

Teams can access coaching and resources related to lean startup, customer discovery, business model canvas, design thinking, and other methodologies and tools utilized by startups and new product development teams to move the idea forward.

At the end of the 3-day stage, the team presents their progress to a group that can help evaluate the evidence and idea brief. This group of evaluators, also known as a growth board or decision board, can consist of business unit leaders, innovation advocates, or people who control the resources needed for the next investment stage. Together they determine whether to invest in the next level of resources to move the idea along (or if it should be pivoted, killed, or shelved). The board will help analyze, monitor, and advise the ideas as they progress through each investment stage.

The growth board serves as a de facto venture capital board that invests via metered funding for resource allocation. Unlike traditional budget funding, metered funding is limited in nature. It mimics the process and cadence a startup would use to seek investment or funding. At each cycle, the innovation team presents to the board, and together they determine whether to continue, pivot, or kill the idea.

The team must come back to the board with progress, data, and traction before receiving additional funding and resources. Teams do not receive further funding unless they can show progress and validated learning.

Metered funding creates a sense of urgency and autonomy for teams and discipline for management. The growth board invests in ideas with resources and capital based on the progress during a stage. The teams have the authority and capability to execute their ideas as needed during the cycle. The initial investment in the idea is much like a seed investment an outside startup would receive. Once "funded," the team works through the initial search phase of discovery, customer development, and market analysis.

4 WEEKS: VALIDATION AND EXPERIMENTS

Ideas that are green-lit to the 4-week stage typically comprise a small, cross-functional team whose job is to build out tests, prototypes, or other customer discovery experiments to further validate the business model's assumptions and build out the idea. At the end of the initial 4 weeks, if the concept continues to show growth, traction, or desired learning, the team can present and request further funding for additional sprints and resources.

The criteria for moving an idea past the 4-week stage will be individually developed and agreed upon with the decision board, looking at specific investment requirements needed to prove the next stage of growth and development.

Each stage is about validating the plan and assumptions, showing evidence of progress, and developing the next steps required to make further investments.

ADDITIONAL KEYS IN THE PROCESS:

- Customer obsessed. Start with the customer and their problems before jumping to solutions.

- Search first vs. execute first. Search for and validate the right plan to implement before executing a plan.

- Be resourceful. Scrounge, borrow, and leverage other departments, people, assets, and networks. Constraints beget creativity. Don't underestimate the scrounging. Think and execute like a startup to move ideas forward.

- Autonomous. Once an idea is green-lit and invested in, teams should have the autonomy to use the resources given as they see fit to develop, execute, and validate the concept until the next stage gate.

- Cross-functional teams. Look for a diverse set of skillsets and perspectives to build out ideas

- Metered funding/incremental investing. Most ideas will not make it through each stage. Be okay with shelving ideas quickly and reallocating resources to other ideas in the pipeline, doubling down on those that show objective evidence of progress.

- Evidence-based progress metrics. Don't rely on hunches or guesses to move an idea forward. Look for external market evidence that you are moving in the right direction.

- Open and collaborative. Share ideas, learnings, failings, and pitfalls early, often, and everywhere.

- Single owner. While multiple people in an ad-hoc group may explore ideas, an accepted idea should have a single person to champion it through the next stage in the process. The owner may change as it moves through the process, but there is always only one.

The 1-2-3-4 process gives individuals and organizations a place to start acting on their ideas. It's a simple way to visualize the execution process and offers a way to right-size the resources and amount of effort at each stage based on evidence and not opinion.

QUICK TAKES TO REMEMBER AND SHARE

- The third engine of innovation is Experimentation. None of the work spent exploring and engaging ideas matters unless you take action to test, try, and transform your ideas into something of value.

- Most ideas begin as a messy bundle of untested assumptions. A good innovation process takes a new idea and de-risks the assumptions along the way.

- To move ideas forward, you must banish the mindset that an idea must be perfect at inception. Treat ideas as guesses or hypotheses to be validated. You can kill, pivot, or shelve ideas based on what you find out.

- Focus on problems first, not solutions. Even better, focus on the big shark bite problems.

- The 1-2-3-4 process is a way to vet ideas while minimizing the risks and resources deployed in the process. It provides a way to research, test, experiment, and move ideas down the path—either tabling those that aren't working or doubling down on those that show evidence, traction, and growth. Each number in the process represents a time box: 1 minute, 2 hours, 3 days, and 4 weeks.

QUICK ACTIONS TO DO NOW

Take an idea you're working on and fill out an idea brief from the chapter. Map out what you know and what evidence you've collected to support the idea. What's missing? What else do you need to explore or collect to give you confidence that your idea is on the right path? What is the next thing you must learn? What can you test to validate if your assumptions are correct? What experiment might you run to find out?

Idea brief template:

- An elevator pitch to describe the opportunity

- Problem statement

- Customer segment(s)

- Market opportunity

- Resources required for the next phase of learning

- Unique insight or special sauce

- Business model canvas (BMC)

CONCLUSION

While we can wish for a stable, predictable future, the truth is we need to embrace uncertainty. Massive technology advancements, shifting market dynamics, and unknown geopolitical and macro-environmental factors guarantee a world filled with endless waves of disruption and opportunity. There are simply too many accelerants to ignore. The speed of change is here to stay, and we must learn skills to thrive in dynamic environments.

Innovation holds the key to unlocking opportunities in unknown environments. The ability to quickly explore, engage, and experiment with new ideas to create new value will set individuals and organizations apart. Those that do will become the Innovation

Accelerators armed with the necessary skills to navigate change and make an impact.

Chapter 1 highlighted the role of the Innovation Accelerator, someone who can take ideas and effectively transform them into reality, and the Accelerator Seven Superpowers of being curious, optimistic, resourceful, resilient, customer driven, action oriented, and collaborative. It also introduced three critical, interconnected engines needed to accelerate innovation: Exploration, Engagement, and Experimentation. These engines enable you to generate ideas, reflect and collaborate, and ultimately act and execute on them. An Innovation Accelerator's job is to fine-tune these engines to make sure ideas move forward faster to create new and valuable outcomes.

Chapter 2 provided the necessary context for the challenges and opportunities driven by today's rapid acceleration of everything from technology to capital to talent. The speed of change and its exponential nature has created an imperative for individuals and organizations to learn new skills, master new mindsets, and prepare for new ways of thriving.

Chapter 3 focused on navigating uncertainty. If we can better adapt to change, today's uncertainty will turn into a massive opportunity. Enabling individual innovators to relinquish and relearn old legacy mindsets, recognizing and rewarding action on new ideas, and defining a vision for innovation were some of the areas explored in the chapter. The chapter covered how to leverage the accelerants of change and outlined a dozen common barriers to accelerating innovation and making it essential everywhere in the organization.

With the proper context of innovation in mind, we set out to provide tactical advice for accelerating your innovation efforts and fine-tuning the three engines of innovation: Exploration, Engagement, and Experimentation. These engines enable you to generate ideas, reflect and collaborate, and ultimately act and execute.

Chapter 4 covered the Exploration Engine, looking at how to seek and gather more ideas, the seeds that can grow to create value. Finding new ideas requires exploration. Exploration is where ideas can begin to collide, merge, and interact. Building out your Exploration Engine is all about accelerating this learning process. The chapter looked at how individuals can amplify their exploration efforts, then offered ways to help organizations do the same with examples like hiring for curiosity, emphasizing learning goals, and letting employees broaden their exposure and interests.

In Chapter 5, we outlined the Engagement Engine and looked at ways to develop and strengthen your collaborative network so that you can quickly engage your ideas with feedback and resources. Engagement is where your ideas collide, mix, and remix. It's where you evaluate, synthesize, and refine your assumptions. Most importantly, it's where you reflect, share, and collaborate with others to sort through and make sense of what's missing and what's not. The Engagement Engine is where you map out your assumptions and begin putting the plans in place to execute and experiment. It's where you engage your ideas to decide what else you need to explore or what next steps are needed to refine, test, or experiment.

Finally, in Chapter 6's discussion of the Experimentation Engine, we offered keys to experimentation and a 1-2-3-4 process to act on an idea. None of the work spent exploring and engaging ideas matters unless you test, try, and transform your ideas into something of value. Most ideas begin as a messy bundle of untested assumptions. A good innovation process takes a new idea and de-risks the assumptions along the way. The 1-2-3-4 process is a way to vet ideas while minimizing the risks and resources deployed. It provides a way to research, test, experiment, and move ideas down the path—either tabling those that aren't working or doubling down on those that show evidence, traction, and growth. Each number in the process represents a time box: 1 minute, 2 hours, 3 days, and 4 weeks.

Now's the time to accelerate your ideas. Now's the time to test, launch, and learn. With the knowledge of the environment and tactics in your toolbox, now's the time to build your innovation competency. Hopefully, this book has given you some insight into the pitfalls and practices for innovating at the speed of change. I hope this book gives you an understanding of the context of innovation in today's uncertain times and a handbook for navigating it faster and more confidently. Armed with the knowledge of the changing landscape of innovation, the barriers and obstacles you'll face, and the powerful engines of innovation, you now have the means to make an impact. Now all you have to do is make a difference.

Thank you for joining me on this journey, and as I say at the end of all my podcasts, go out and innovate!

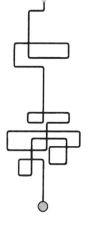

ACKNOWLEDGMENTS

I'd first like to thank everyone out there who bought, borrowed, read, skimmed, or shared a copy of this book. I'm so grateful to those who took the time to learn, grow, and build on the journey with me.

To our fantastic community of builders, makers, movers, shakers, creators, and doers within the Inside Outside community: I've grown so much from all our interactions and the time we've spent together. To the startups and corporate teams who I've worked with, invested in, or observed up close, thank you for sharing your ups, downs, and in-betweens.

Thank you to the many, many experts, mentors, and colleagues I've had the privilege to work with and learn from—including Janice Fraser, David Bland, Diana Kander, Alex Osterwalder, Tendayi Viki, Chris Shipley, Tristan Kromer, Justin Wilcox, Lorrie Vogel, Amy Radin, Jeff Gothelf, Josh Seiden, Barry O'Reilly, Alistair Croll, Ben Yoskovitz, Rita McGrath, Steve Case, Brad Feld, Paul Singh, Tyler Crowley, April Rinne, Sean Ammirati, Jack Elkins, Neil Soni, Brant Cooper, Josh Linkner, and Seth Godin.

No book can be written without a healthy dose of unconditional love and support from family and friends. Thank you, Mom, Dad, Nick, John, Chris, Tom, Sharon, Carla, Gary, Shannon, and Phil. And most importantly, thank you to my amazing wife, Susan Stibal. She is my partner in life and business, and none of what I do would be remotely possible without her. And finally, thank you to my kiddos, Lily and Bodie, for allowing me to be a crazy dad. I love you beyond words.

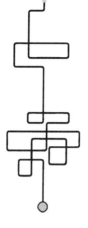

ABOUT THE AUTHOR

Brian is the founder of Inside Outside, a community for entrepreneurs, innovators, and anyone interested in accelerating new ideas. Brian publishes a weekly podcast, newsletter, and annual event series, while also serving as Director of Innovation at Nelnet. For over twenty-five years, Brian has been helping entrepreneurs and enterprises navigate and compete in a world of change and disruption. He has led efforts between startups and corporates to engage the latest trends, tools, and tactics to accelerate innovation, launch new ideas, and build better products.

Previously, Brian founded the seed-stage accelerator NMotion and co-founded the corporate innovation consultancy Econic. Brian was Chief Marketing Officer at Nanonation, working with clients including Pepsi, Target, Nike, Mazda, Harley-Davidson, and Royal Caribbean. Brian built out the consulting arm in Asia for Gartner and worked with technology giants including Microsoft, IBM, and HP. He also led Asia's first dedicated customer experience lab as head of research at Ion Global, a Hong Kong–headquartered technology firm.

Brian has been a champion of the Midwest startup and innovation ecosystem through his work with programs such as Startup Champions Network, gener8tor, Lean Startup Circle, Pipeline Entrepreneurs, Startup Weekend, Nebraska Tech Collaborative, Rise of the Rest, Startup Week, UP Global, Nebraska Angels, and the JumpStart Challenge.

Brian is a regular contributor to industry publications, a public speaker, and quoted industry expert with over two decades of experience in digital media, marketing, consulting, and research. He holds a bachelor's degree in marketing from the University of Nebraska at Omaha and an MBA from Penn State. Brian makes his home in Lincoln, Nebraska with his amazing wife, Susan Stibal, and their two talented children, Lily and Bodie.